MAKE EVERY DAY
A WINSDAY

FREDDY FRI

Print: ISBN - 978-1-7347471-0-2

DEDICATION

To my mother, Theresa Frierson
Words cannot express how much you are missed!
Thanks so much for always being my guardian angel!

To my father, Fred Frierson Sr,
Thanks so much for stepping up and raising me
to become the man that I am today!

To my wife, Lisa Frierson
Thank you for being my rock and always
pushing and supporting me! I love you!

To my children, Destinee, Brittany, Kendrick and Shae
Thank you for being my reasons and my why!
Each one of you gave me purpose and the strength
to never give up!

TABLE OF CONTENTS

INTRODUCTION

I Could Never Have Imagined

As an innocent four-year-old child watching my mama's casket being closed, I could never have imagined . . .

As I fought to breathe while they held my head under water and tried to drown me, I could never have imagined . . .

As I struggled to overcome shyness and the fear of performing on stage, I could never have imagined . . .

As I hid in the corner of my attic from the police beating on my front door, I could never have imagined . . .

As I prayed and prayed that my life would not be spent behind prison bars, I could never have imagined . . .

As the tears of life's failures streamed down my face, I could never have imagined . . .

I couldn't imagine living a successful life. I couldn't imagine turning the burdens of my life into a positive legacy. I couldn't imagine turning my losing ways into positivity and winning. Mostly, I could never have imagined that I would be writing this book. I firmly believe that everyone has a story to tell. Uplifting stories of overcoming life's obstacles are necessary and should be shared with the masses. These types of stories provide inspiration and helps give others the courage to conquer their fears. For these reasons, I am sharing my story with you. By the grace of God and my guardian angel (whom you will learn more about later), I overcame.

If you're reading this book, you are probably at a crossroads in your life. You may feel that success is unachievable. Or, you may feel that you're below average. Some may feel that they are downright losers with no purpose in life. Those feelings couldn't be further from the truth! You see, I have experienced those same feelings and haven't always made the best decisions. Although I have suffered countless pitfalls, I never lost sight of my goals. I prayed and believed for better days. Rather than giving up, I planned and strategized an exit from the enormous pit that I dug for myself. In due course, I emerged from that deep pit victorious and a much better person.

As you read about my trials and failures, it will become apparent that most of them were self-inflicted. There were many things that I could have done differently to elicit a better outcome. However, I lacked the maturity and discipline to make the best decisions for my life. In the end, I acknowledged all of my messes and made the necessary adjustments to rectify them. My life now is purposeful and with clear direction. I continue to strive in making every day of my life a "WINSday."

I hope my story empowers you to look beyond any missteps that you have made. Know that you are an overcomer with the power and capacity to be successful. Failure is never an option! It is of utmost importance to never give up on your dreams. The universe will grant you as many favors as you need, but it takes its cues from you. Once you begin taking positive action, things will inexplicably happen in your favor. Therefore, sit back, relax and fasten your seatbelts as you join me on this roller coaster ride of my life. Although the ride is bumpy, it's filled with a variety of methods for defeating adversity. Using our internal global positioning system (GPS), we will arrive at the destination of next-level! Welcome to my life, my story and enjoy the ride!

CHAPTER

(Mama Gone)

"Life is tough when you're missing mama"
"As a boy I remember I was wishing mama"
"Wake up thought you was sleeping hope you listen mama"
"Hear my cries I can't remember even kissing mama"
Lyrics taken from verse 1 of
Playya 1000 and The Deeksta's song "Mama"
(Full song available on all streaming platforms)

Three years ago while sitting in my office, I pondered all of the ups and down of my life. I was feeling especially proud of my successful transformation from boy to man and prevailing against the trials of life. In that moment, I knew that I wanted to share my story with the world. Excited about my personal evolution, I needed to share with others that success is real and achievable no matter the circumstances. From the reflections of my life and all of its pitfalls, my "Make Every Day a WINSday" videos were borne.

Much like a child eagerly waiting to open Christmas day presents, I was filled with enthusiasm. You see, I was preparing to record my next "Make Every Day a WINSday" video. Just as I was about to profess: "lights, camera and action," one of the camera lights went dim. Without a fully lit background, recording a quality video would be nearly impossible. This was a staunch reminder that I should have grabbed the camera charger from my bedroom prior to recording the video. In a single action, as if I was the great Olympic sprinter Usain Bolt, I sprinted downstairs to my bedroom to grab the charger. Upon entering the room, looking dazed and out of breath, I found my wife sitting on the bed watching television. She took one inquisitive look at me, shook her head and laughed. She said, "There you go again, running around like a chicken with your head cut off!"

I have a tendency of rushing around the house like "ninety to nothing" whenever working on my videos. Teasing me about rushing around the house, my wife proceeded to mimic my actions. Imagine her hurriedly running throughout the house from room to room. She goes from the bedroom to the kitchen, bathroom, living room and back to bedroom where she started. All the while, she is imitating how I appear when trying to do fifty things at once. While acting this out, she repeats the words "pow, pow, pow" repetitively; and hits the walls with the palms of her hands. She says that's her interpretation of the explosions of information going on in my head. Her academy award winning performance is quite hilarious. After her rendition of the "method to my madness," we both fell on the bed and had a gut-busting laugh about it. At that very moment, I glanced up and saw Queen Latifah on the television screen.

Most people know Queen Latifah as a successful actress and television show host. However, she is also one of the original female rappers of hip-hop. Queen Latifah is also a national recording artist. She has sold millions of records, graced the covers of countless magazines and a plethora of fans have watched her music videos. She is widely recognized by the legendary title of queen of hip-hop. Basically, she is what we call "big time." Early in my own hip-hop career, I was graced with the opportunity to perform in the same show with Queen Latifah. The show was held in Oklahoma City, Oklahoma, which is close to my hometown of Tulsa, Oklahoma.

Playya 1000 and The Deeksta is the name of my rap group. We were up and coming rap artists during that time and we opened the show. That night, we had a phenomenal performance. The crowd was enthralled with our set and we felt the energy. Coming off the stage from our performance, I was amped up. Adrenaline was rushing throughout my body, and I was full of excitement. Things could not have gone any better for me that day, or so I thought. What happened next landed me on cloud nine. As I looked to my left, I saw none other than the queen herself. Queen Latifah was standing right in front of me! I tried to keep my cool, but felt like I was going to pass out. I was definitely star struck! She looked me directly in the eyes, gave the biggest smile and said, "Bro, y'all had 'em rockin!" Meaning, she felt like the crowd really enjoyed our performance. I tried to maintain my composure, but I was completely mesmerized by her presence. At that time, she had a starring role in the popular television show, Living Single. I felt like I was actually in an episode of Living Single with her. The moment was surreal, one I will never forget.

Intrigued by Queen Latifah in the movie that my wife was watching, I completely forgot about the camera charger. I asked my wife what she was watching and she replied "Steel Magnolias." She was viewing the remake of the original version that starred Sally Field, Dolly Parton, and Julia Roberts. In the remake version, Queen Latifah had a starring role alongside Phylicia Rashad and Alfre Woodard, who is a Tulsa native like myself. I had never seen the original version so this movie really caught my attention. It was even more interesting being that Queen Latifah was a cast member. My wife explained that the movie was about a newly married young lady who wanted to have a child of her own. However, she had some medical problems and her doctor advised that she not have any children. She was told that a pregnancy would threaten her life and the life of her unborn child. Against the wishes of her doctor and family, the young lady became pregnant. Even though there were grave concerns about her pregnancy, she eventually delivered a healthy baby boy.

Unfortunately, as her physician had anticipated, the young lady suffered severe kidney damage because of the pregnancy. Sadly, when her son was just a toddler, she suddenly passed away. I was completely numb while watching this movie. It closely paralleled the plight of my mother, Theresa Frierson. Upon realizing the similarities between the movie and my own story, I was overcome with emotion. Through it all, my wife was there. She gave me a gentle hug as tears of missing my mother rolled down my face.

Located in Southeastern Oklahoma, Hugo is a small town with a population of about five thousand people. This is the town my mom called home. She was the light of our family. She was full of life and laughter. While in her twenties, my mother fell ill and went to the local doctor for treatment. Unbeknownst to her, she was misdiagnosed and given medication that damaged her kidneys. Just like in the movie, Steel Magnolias, my mother's doctor advised her to never become pregnant in fear of further damage to her organs. The doctor told her that if she became pregnant, it would threaten her life and mine.

My mom desperately wanted to have a child of her own and that is exactly what happened. To mother's delight, I was conceived. I am told that she was filled with extreme happiness and joy. However, others did not share the exhilaration. Her doctor and family members told her to abort me for her own safety. She steadfastly refused to agree to an abortion. Her mind was made up; she was going to have me and believed that everything would be okay. Actually, everything was okay for a while. I was born whole and healthy. I am told that my mother was very happy about having her baby boy. I was her miracle. My mother experienced a few blissful years of motherhood before getting her angel wings. When I was just four years old, she was called to be with the Lord. Still, she is deeply missed.

Although recollections of my mother are foggy, I do have three vivid memories of her. The first memory is of her protective arms that kept me from being burned along with my father. As he often did, my father was at home working on his motorcycle in the garage. I loved watching my dad work on his cars and motorcycle. He would always let me sit on the porch near him and watch. One day in particular, he was working on his motorcycle when it caught on fire. I don't remember how it happened, but flames engulfed the motorcycle and his clothing. Out of nowhere, my mother hoisted me off the porch away from the flames. After that, she began extinguishing the blazing fire from my dad. She was a courageous woman. She saved my dad's life and mine. Although my dad survived the ordeal, he suffered extensive burns to his body. I am happy to say that over the course of time, he fully recovered from his injuries.

In my second memory, daddy was driving mama to the hospital because she fell ill. I was sitting in the back seat of the car watching her. She was grimacing in pain and guarding her abdomen. At my age, I didn't exactly know what was happening, but I knew something was not right. That car ride to the hospital would be the last time and place that I would share with my mother on this earth. Daddy was able to get her to the hospital while she was still alive, but it was still too late. Shortly thereafter, she passed away.

The third and most powerful memory of my mother is her funeral. Again, I was only four years old so I didn't understand why so many people were walking up to her casket crying. I didn't even know what a casket was nor did I know that I was attending her funeral. I just remember thinking to myself, *why is everyone crying over my mom?* Reflecting back, I now understand that my family was paying their respects to her and mourning her loss. My personal mourning of her loss would come at a much later time.

Growing up, I missed mama so much. I often wished that I could hear her voice or feel her motherly touch. I grappled with the absence of my mother during the major milestones of my life. This left a deep void in my soul for a long period of time. Honestly, I don't even remember kissing mama. However, I know she loved me with all of her being. I also know without a doubt that she is my guardian angel watching over and protecting me. It's uncanny how so many complicated situations have seemed to spontaneously resolve in my favor over my life. I believe it is the essence of my mother's spirit that has provided me a shield from harm. Thinking of her always put a big, bright smile on my face.

Because I was a young child when my mother passed away, I never really mourned her loss until I became an adult. I always thought a proper mourning would occur at the gravesite or through a family celebration of her life. Yet, neither of those situations happened. Instead, my fellow students joined me in honoring the memory of my mother. I was taking a public speaking class in college and my assignment was to write a commemorative speech. It was a seemingly regular day and everything was going as planned. Standing at the podium, I was thrilled to be completing the speech as an ode to my mom.

In the beginning, my speech was going well and my classmates were engaged. However, as I began to speak about the events surrounding my mother's death and funeral, I became filled with emotion. The more I spoke, the closer the tears came to dropping from my eyes. I told myself, *you can't cry in front of all these people.* I desperately tried to fight back the tears, but I knew my levee was about to break. There was literally nothing I could do about it in that moment. Therefore, I decided to stop fighting my emotions and allowed it to release. By the end of my speech, there was not a dry eye in the room. It was such a powerful, cathartic moment. It was also in that moment that the realization came over me that I had not ever truly mourned my mother's passing. It was all the more meaningful to have the love and support of my classmates and instructor during that time. It was amazing to have them join me in honoring my mother. That day will always be remembered. From my personal experience with death and loss, I would encourage healthy mourning and release of emotions. This greatly helped my personal growth and mental well-being.

CHAPTER

2

(Me, Pops and My Step Mom)

"Now it's me and pops as a team"
"But papa was a rolling stone, know what I mean"
"Got a step mama that I wanna smoke"
"Treat me like dirt cause my pops on the go"
"In and out when he's gone ain't no tellin how she act"
"Come to find out my step ma smoking crack"
Lyrics taken from verse 1 of
Playya 1000 and The Deeksta's song
"Love Don't Live Here"
(Full song available on all streaming platforms)

I was born and raised in the heart of North Tulsa, Oklahoma.
Tulsa in general is a beautiful city. However, life on the Northside
is all about the survival of the fittest on any given day. You grow
up fast and learn the ways of the world at a young age. Many
of the people who reside in North Tulsa live below the federal

7

poverty level. Certain sections of North Tulsa are stricken with high crime and gang activity. Growing up, I've had many friends who have been murdered, seriously hurt or ended up serving prison time. Basically, North Tulsa is considered the ghetto. Or, as some would say, it's the "hood." Even so, I called it home.

In my neck of the woods, it was rare to see a father in the home. Most of the households were ran by mothers while fathers were absent. Single parent homes managed by the female seemed normal. In communities like mine, if a mother was deemed unfit to care for her children or had passed away, the children were typically sent to live with another female relative. It was not unusual for an aunt or grandmother to raise orphaned children. Sadly, in some cases, foster care was the only option. I consider myself one of the lucky ones. When my mother passed away, my father did not shirk his responsibilities. I was not sent away to live with a female relative as many are. Instead, my father remained a part of my life and has always been supportive. Thankfully, my father embraced his duties as a man and as a father. So, it became me and pops as a team. He was a part of my life in everything I did. For that, I am eternally grateful.

As a young boy, I loved and worshipped my dad. He was my idol. He did his very best in providing and caring for me. I'm sure he never imagined that he would become a single father. In my situation, rather than the female being the primary caretaker, my father filled those shoes. Unlike many residents of North Tulsa, we lived relatively well because my father worked incessantly. It seemed like he was always at work. That commitment to his work kept me clothed, clean, and properly fed. However, it was hard on him working long hours and raising a child alone. He needed more help with raising me. During this time is when my stepmom entered the picture. .

I was just a young boy when they began their relationship. In my six year old mind, it seemed like she came out of nowhere and became part of our family. Suddenly, she was just there living in our house. This marked the moment that pops and I were no longer a team of two. It became me, pops and my stepmom.

Initially, I liked her just fine. My youthfulness had not allowed me to see her for the person that she really was. As I grew older, I quickly began to realize that my home life was far from ideal.

In my neighborhood, there was a grocery store called "Best Yet." Although the name suggests differently, there was nothing particularly special about it. The building was old and in need of a facelift. There was also a lot of loitering around the building. Yet, I was proud that we had a neighborhood store. At least we had access to fresh produce and not just junk foods like other sections of North Tulsa. Best Yet was my favorite store as a kid. I loved going there with my dad on shopping trips.

Not too long after becoming part of our family, my stepmom began forcing me to walk to Best Yet to buy her cigarettes. You heard me right; I did say buy cigarettes as a child. At that time, the laws did not preclude kids from buying cigarettes. And, I absolutely hated it! Like it was yesterday, I remember her cigarette brand of choice was Kool Filter Kings. We lived close enough to the store that I could walk along the trail leading from the back of my house to the back of the store. Essentially, it was a short-cut to the store. Unwillingly, I walked to that store and bought cigarettes countless times. It's an unthinkable story, but true. I often think back about how crazy it sounds that I legally bought cigarettes as a kid. Thankfully, several years later, laws were enacted to prevent the sale of tobacco products to children.

My stepmom had two kids of her own before she and my dad eventually had a child together. The children she had before meeting my dad did not consistently live with us. I found that to be very strange. They visited our home at times, but lived regularly with their paternal grandmother in a different city. As I got older, I often wondered how my stepmom could act like she was my mother when she didn't even take care of her own children. Her relationship with my dad was often turbulent. Looking back on those times, I feel she displaced much of her anger towards my father onto me. In part, that is why she treated me so badly.

My dad loved to gamble. Once a month, he would host a card game at our house and invite several of his friends. I loved when they had those card games because that meant he was home. When all of his friends were around, my stepmom projected a fake personality. She acted friendly and went to great lengths to be nice. When she acted that way, I always thought something was wrong with her. I knew her conniving ways and could see right through the fakeness. However, during my dad's card games, she was on her best behavior. Daddy's card games were the best. His friends were hilarious and they all had funny nicknames. I used to laugh and get a kick out of watching and listening to their animation. They would pay me to get food and drinks from the kitchen. That was just a part of my dad's lifestyle and very fun times for me.

My living situation changed when I was eight years old. For some unknown reason, I was sent to live temporarily with my aunt in Hugo, Oklahoma. As aforementioned, Hugo is the town where my mother was born and raised. Actually, both of my parents grew up in the small town of Hugo and many of my family members from both sides still live there. This particular aunt with whom I temporarily lived was not my mother's sister, but she is my dad's sibling. Her name is Trudy Anne, better known as "Aunt Trudanne." Everyone in our family pronounces her name as one word with all of the letters running together, like a lot of country folk do. I absolutely loved my Aunt "Trudanne." Although she had five kids of her own, she took care of me like I was her sixth child. She never made me feel like I was anything less than her own child. I'll always love and respect her for that.

Grandma Gertrude also lived in Hugo. I spent a lot of time at her home when I lived with Aunt "Trudanne." Grandma Gertrude is my paternal grandmother. I loved being at her house. I'd go over there and we would watch her favorite soap operas and *The Price is Right*. Nobody was allowed to bother my grandmother when she was watching her favorite television shows except for me. I felt like I was her favorite grandchild. I was just really comfortable in Hugo; it was a cool, small town environment. I had lots of friends and really enjoyed my time there. I had forgotten all about the drama and problems that went on at home in Tulsa. During my second and third grade years, I lived in Hugo. By fourth grade, I moved home back to Tulsa. For a reason I don't recall, I went back to Hugo to live for my fifth grade year. By sixth grade, I was back home in Tulsa for good.

Upon returning home for good in sixth grade, I was no longer a young boy. I was a pre-teen and had begun to view life differently. At that time, the harsh realities of my stepmom became even more apparent. She was unbelievably hateful for absolutely no reason. I wanted to like her, but couldn't. It was obvious that she was mentally broken and full of anger. Unfortunately for me, I was often the target of her frustrations. Most likely, there were past hurts that she endured, which shaped the way she acted towards others. To worsen matters, I learned that she had a drinking problem. It seemed like she drank every day, which made her even more mean-spirited.

It didn't seem like my home life could get any worse, but it did. My stepmom eventually began smoking crack cocaine. My dad was hardly ever home because he still worked a lot of hours. My stepmom was pretty much able to have free reign at home and she was an absolute terror! She didn't try to hide any of her alcohol or drug habits around me. I would tell my dad about the horrendous things going on in our home when he wasn't there. It seemed like he was listening, but I don't believe he fully understood the magnitude of the situation.

One evening, my younger brother and I were lying in bed to go to sleep for the night. All of a sudden, my stepmom yelled for us to come into her bedroom. We quickly jumped out of bed and went to her room. She told us that she had some very bad news. Coldly, she told us that our dad had died. My brother and I were completely devastated. We were crying uncontrollably and couldn't believe what we were hearing. She let us cry for a while without saying a word. I guess our tears were eventually too much for her to handle. Because she then calmly told us that our dad actually wasn't dead. She admitted that she made up the entire story. We didn't know what to believe. To prove to us that he wasn't really dead, she called him at work so we could hear his voice. With total relief, we were able to speak with our dad and verify that he was still alive. What my stepmom had done is one of the cruelest things someone could do to a child. But, things like that that happened all the time. It got to the point where you just never knew what was going to happen next. I was very afraid of her.

My stepmom's two other children would live with us periodically. One night, we all had eaten dinner and were playing around and having fun. My stepmom seemed to be in an extra foul mood, even more than usual. Because she was being indifferent, we were all ordered to go to bed early with the exception of her daughter. My stepmom directed her daughter to clean the house. Not just one room; the entire house! My stepsister was kept up all night cleaning various rooms of the house. All the while, my stepmom was yelling at her, degrading her with profanity-laced rants and hurling continuous insults. My brothers and I counted that our sister was called the "b-word" a total of forty-three times that night. I felt very sorry her. She didn't deserve that type of treatment. It was very inappropriate and disrespectful. I completely understood why her two eldest children would rarely come stay with us. When it came to being hateful, with the exception of my younger brother, my stepmom didn't discriminate. Her daughter and I caught the brunt of her wrath.

Back when there were no cellphones and landlines were common, I would sneak on the phone and call a girl I liked after I thought my stepmom had gone to sleep. We had phones in the living room, kitchen, and my parents' room. There was very little privacy with landlines. Anyone could easily pick up the phone line from another room and listen in on the conversation. This particular night, I was talking to this young lady who I admired very much. All of a sudden, I heard my stepmom's drunken voice on the line. She said "Who is this little b---h you're on the phone talking to"? I thought my stepmom was sleeping. She took me by total surprise. I was instantly embarrassed and quickly hung the phone up on my lady friend. I wished I had the courage to confront my stepmom about her foul behavior. However, I never talked back to her because of the fear she instilled in me.

By the time I reached high school, I wasn't as fearful of my stepmom as before. And, neither was her daughter for that matter. After a day of hanging out with my friends, I came home to an argument between my stepmom and her daughter. When I reached them, they were "touching furniture," meaning, they were fighting. I quickly intervened and broke up their tussle. I guess my stepmom had started one of her normal, abusive rants and her daughter decided that she had just had enough. Part of me felt like I should have let the daughter beat her up. Yet, I knew that wasn't right. In spite of her hateful ways, I could never see myself fighting her. All I wanted to do was graduate from high school, get my own place, and be rid of her forever. That eventually happened, but not without incident.

While I was still in high school, my stepmom was on one of her drunken rampages again. She began pushing me around and making disparaging remarks. I attempted to walk away but she kept putting her hands on me and yelling louder. Before I knew it, I snapped. I grabbed her and put her in a headlock. I remember saying over and over again, "I'm sick of you! I'm tired of you! I hate you!" I was just about to completely lose it when I caught myself. I quickly regained my composure and ran out of the house. My heart was racing, I couldn't hardly catch my breath, and I was on the verge of crying. In that moment, I had a revelation. I needed to find a way to forgive her before I did something that I would regret forever. Earnestly, I asked for God's forgiveness and in turn, I forgave her.

Let it be known that there will always be people in your life who will do things to hurt you. That hurt may be inadvertent or purposeful. No matter the intent, you must forgive. The forgiveness is not for them, but for yourself. You must entirely forgive them to gain full healing of your heart and soul. In addition, forgiving someone doesn't mean that the relationship has to be restored, especially if it was toxic. Forgiveness does not equal restoration! You can forgive and move on from a relationship rather than restoring it. Even as I forgave my stepmom, I knew that we would never have a close bond. Afterwards, our relationship changed for the better in the sense that there were no more altercations. We found a way to be cordial with one another. We still aren't close by any means and we rarely speak or see one another. However, I know that my choice to forgive her was imperative to my progression in life. Never let anyone take your power. Forgiveness will set you free from mental, psychological and emotional bondage.

CHAPTER

(Shy, Smart and Bullied)

"Cut off jeans"
"Bottle soda pops, young, but I had big dreams"
"Walk the halls fifth grade, hope they notice me"
"They used to bully I would run when they were approaching me"
"Just a face in the crowd"
"Shy boy, hoop dreams never said out loud"
Lyrics taken from verse 1 of
Playya 1000 and The Deeksta's song "Dreams"
(Full song available on all streaming platforms)

Although I endured much craziness and drama at home, I excelled at academics. I was naturally book smart and schoolwork was relatively easy for me. I was a straight "A" student throughout school. Unlike some other students, I enjoyed attending classes. Funny thing is that I never studied much and rarely had homework. In many ways, I was sort of a nerdy kid but at the same time, not so nerdy (if there is such a thing). I was also good at operating electronic equipment at an early age. If there was a piece of equipment not working properly, I could usually figure out how to fix it. I count all of these things as my blessings and personal gifts in life.

Being that I was an exemplary student, I was often selected by teachers to answer questions in class. Even though I knew the correct answer to most questions, I loathed being picked in class to give an answer. I was terribly shy and introverted. Speaking in front of others was one of my worst fears. Anxiety would ensue, I would start shaking and panic would set in. Therefore, whenever I was picked to answer a question or read aloud, I would always try to find a way to avoid it. If I were unable to circumvent the question, I would always speak in a very soft, low tone of voice. It was so low that teachers would always tell me to speak louder so everyone could hear. As gifted as I was, that was very difficult for me to do. However, I did not seem to have the same problem communicating when it came to sports.

Playing and watching sports were some of my greatest enjoyments. To this day, I still love watching sports. I have always been a huge football fan. I loved Sunday NFL football, especially the Dallas Cowboys. They were my favorite team and I watched them religiously. I also loved playing football. As a kid, I aspired to be a football or basketball star. I used to play wide receiver. I loved catching passes and faking people out; I had great hands. Whenever we played street football, I would always be one of the first picks on a team. I was short, but I had an uncanny knack for catching any pass thrown my way. One time, I remember being so engaged and focused on trying to catch a pass that I ran smack dab into the back of a parked truck. The impact almost knocked me out. I most likely suffered a concussion but in those days, you just got up and kept playing. That is, if you could. When I came to my senses, all I wanted to know was if I had caught the ball.

Playing basketball was also a great love of mine. With a select group of friends, I often played basketball in my backyard. We regularly played three on three or four on four. We had so much fun and the competitiveness was amazing. I also played organized basketball in school. When I was in elementary, I played for a team called the William Penn All Stars. We were one of the best teams in our area. One of my teammates would eventually go on to play in the NBA. Although I was the sixth man on our team, I got a lot of playing time. I had a lot of heart for the game and understood how to play the game well. I was always the vocal leader on our team, or what some call "the coach on the floor". I loved playing defense and directing my team on where they should be positioned during a game. Whether I was playing organized basketball or street ball in my backyard, I just simply loved the sport. My friends and I had many fun times playing on my basketball goal. However, there were a few times when things were not so pleasant.

It started in my own backyard, on my own basketball court. One day, my friends and I were having fun playing each other when a group of older boys came into my backyard unannounced. Before we knew it, the older boys grabbed my basketball and pushed us aside. They took over my goal and our game and just started playing. Remember, I lived in the hood so this type of scenario is not unheard of. In a nutshell, they were plain old bullies. I was very upset but my dad was not home, so I could not run and tell him. I did not know what to do. The older boys, who seemed more like grown men, were rubbing it in our faces. They kept dunking on my goal even after I pleaded for them to stop. They were being very rough and boisterous. At one point, one of the boys jumped what seemed like 20 feet in the air and made a ferocious dunk on my goal. His dunk destroyed my backboard. The rim was completely pulled off the backboard. I remember just sitting there steaming mad and crying while they laughed and ran away. That day, I felt so weak. I felt like I could not do anything to protect myself. I remember just wishing my dad was home, but unfortunately, he was at work. There was nothing any of us could do. Sadly, this was not my only experience with being bullied.

One year during Halloween, I had just been trick-or-treating with a couple of friends. There were three of us boys in total.

The mother of one friend was our chaperone. We went door-to-door getting candy and our bags were full. As darkness set in, my friend's mom brought us all back to their house. Since me and the other friend lived close by, our chaperone figured it would be safe for us to walk home together. Instead of us going straight home as we were instructed, we got greedy and decided to go trick-or-treating for more candy. As we were walking, we noticed a group of older boys behind us. They were moving faster and faster towards us. Realizing that they were coming after us, we also started walking faster. I distinctly remember looking over at my friend and saying, "They're about to try and snatch our bags." In other words, they were about to try to take our candy. We took off running as fast as we could. I was ahead of my friend and remember yelling for him to catch up. He couldn't keep up so I ran behind a house and hid underneath a car. They were too fast for my friend; they caught up with him, took his candy and beat him up. I felt so bad. After they attacked him, they came looking for me. They figured out my hiding spot and drug me from underneath the car. Then, they snatched my pumpkin container of candy, and punched me in the stomach before finally running off. I remember thinking about how I couldn't wait to get older, stronger and wiser, so that I wouldn't have to deal with bullying anymore.

The events that took place on Halloween were nothing compared to the worst incident of bullying I endured. One day, I was walking home from school. I had taken a shortcut through the school playground when three guys started chasing me. I took off running as fast as I could. It felt like my heart was going to pound right through my chest. Eventually, they caught up with me. I was picked up like a sack of potatoes and body slammed to the ground. They punched me several times before dragging me to a nearby swimming pool. The gate around the swimming pool was locked but someone had cut a hole in the fence. My perpetrators pulled me through the hole in the fence as I tried to fight them off. Once we were inside the fence, they pulled me into the water and held me under. They were trying to drown me! I feared that I was about to die. I tried to break free by throwing my arms around and flailing but nothing worked. Just as I thought my life was over, they pulled my head up from the water. I was hyperventilating and trying to catch my breath. While I was fighting for my life, they laughed as if it was no big deal. They then hopped out of the pool and ran away. For a while, I just sat there in the water, drenched and defeated. I couldn't stop crying. It was one of the lowest points in my life. I felt extremely helpless, hopeless, and embarrassed.

Instead of simply getting out of the pool and walking home, I took a moment to sit up on the side of the rail. I said to myself, *this is the last time that anymore bullying is going to happen to me.* I was determined that those same guys were going to respect me one day. I didn't know how it was going to happen but I knew it would happen. I asked God to show me a sign, to give me strength and to help me find a way to be stronger. I prayed that those who bullied me would one day respect me. Afterwards, a feeling of infinite peace came over me. I vowed never to be bullied again, to develop a strong inner strength, and to position myself to be respected not only throughout my community but also throughout the world.

CHAPTER

4

(Hip Hop Saved My Life)

"Shy boy hoop dreams the world is so cold"
"They used to bully me and then I finally struck gold"
"One, two and you don't stop"
"I fell in love when I got introduced to Hip-Hop"
Lyrics taken from verse 1 of
Playya 1000 and The Deeksta's song "Believe in You"
(Full song available on all streaming platforms)

Sometimes your saving grace comes not only when you least expect it, but it may also manifest in a form that you never imagined. I have been an avid sports fan my entire life. I loved watching and playing different sports. I figured my major breakthrough in life would be a result of being involved in sports related activities. Like many young boys, I dreamt of making it to the NBA or NFL. I was athletically inclined and knew that either one of these organizations could change my life forever. Yet, I also loved music to the core of my being. Different beats, melodies and musical notes excited me. My favorite singers included pop artists like Michael Jackson, Prince, The Bee Gees, and the Doobie Brothers. There was a point in time when I actually thought I was Michael McDonald, the lead singer of the Doobie Brothers. His voice was deep and rich. It was unique and nothing like I had ever heard before. *Minute-by-Minute* was a popular song recorded by the Doobie Brothers and Michael McDonald was the lead singer. When that song was on, I would pretend to be Michael McDonald himself. I knew all of the words and could not wait to sing along. While sitting on the side of the couch in the living room, I would perform my best rendition of Michael McDonald. I would pretend to play a piano and sing along in my fabricated deep voice. My friends would get a big kick out of watching me imitate Michael McDonald. By the time I was done, they all would be on the floor laughing so hard. Although sports was a significant part of my life, music deeply penetrated my soul. My saving grace turned out to have nothing to do with sports. It came in the form of music.

As I grew older, my taste for music begin to change. There was a new art form of music that emerged in the 1970s and went global by the 1980s. It was called hip-hop. It started as an underground pastime and became a worldwide sensation. I will admit, I was in awe of hip-hop music. "Rappers Delight" by the Sugarhill Gang is the very first rap song I recall hearing. Everybody loved it, including myself. I knew every word of the song. Everyone in my hood knew all of the lyrics too. The song was very popular. It penetrated my entire community. Even though I was completely enamored with hip-hop music, I still considered sports to be my number one passion. That is, until I discovered a group called Run DMC.

One night, I was up late watching one of the few channels available on TV. That is when I came across a show called *Night Tracks.* This was one of the first music video programs broadcasted in my area. That night, they played a song called "Rock Box" by Run DMC. When I heard that song, my life went into a full 360-degree orbit. To say that I was captivated is an understatement. I totally lost it! I was unbelievably fascinated with that song and the group. No doubt, I had become the number one Run DMC fan! At that exact moment, I knew what I wanted to do with my life. I wanted to become a rap star and a DJ, just like the group Run DMC with Jam Master Jay. There were three members in Run DMC. Two were rappers and one was a DJ. The rappers were known as Run and DMC. Jam Master Jay was the DJ and he mixed the beats. In order to be like Run DMC, I needed music equipment. Thus, I begged my dad to buy me a turntable, mixer and microphone. When he agreed, I lost my mind!

Immediately, I started rewriting Run DMC raps. They had a song called *King of Rock* so I wrote a song called *King of Rap*. I was rewriting their lyrics in my own words. I was beyond excited. However, there was one small problem. I was still very shy and my stage fright had not improved at all. I knew that I would not be able to perform or share my newfound passion with others outside the four walls of my home. The only people who knew I could write lyrics and rap were my closest friends. I reasoned that I could just continue having fun with writing and performing my lyrics without the audience. I had no real intentions of sharing my music with the outside world. Fortunately, another saving grace changed the trajectory of my rap career. His name was Ernest Walker.

Ernest Walker was a friend of mine. He lived about a block from my home. Ernest knew that I liked to rap and he had the bright idea of asking me to try-out for an upcoming talent show at school. A pivotal moment in my life occurred when Ernest came to my home unannounced and asked the unthinkable. He said "Man, I know you have music equipment and I know you're writing raps. They're having a talent show at school and you should enter it with me." I responded, "You mean I would have to get on stage in front of people and rap"? Ernest replied "Yes"! You know how to write raps and you have all of the necessary music equipment. You can do it!" I emphatically said "No sir! I am not getting on stage in front of anybody. These raps and my equipment are for my own personal use. I'm fine recording music at home, behind my closed doors"! While speaking those words, feelings of embarrassment and failure rose inside me as I reflected on a previous time in junior high school when I tried out for the school talent show. I was part of a lip-syncing trio. We attempted to lip-sync a rap song, but failed miserably. We didn't even make the final cut. That experience killed my confidence and was still haunting me. I was determined to never let that happen again. If that meant avoiding any live performances, I was willing to accept that as my plight. At least, that is what I thought. Truth be told, deep down inside I really wanted to be part of the talent show. I secretly had dreams of becoming a rap superstar, but my shyness and fear of being on stage were crippling. Consequently, I gave Ernest one final "no" and thought that would be the end of the conversation.

To my benefit, Ernest did not listen to a word I said. He kept telling me that I could do exactly what I thought I could not. It's a blessing when someone sees something in you that you don't see in yourself. I was fortunate that Ernest remained persistent, and found a way to override my resistance. Without fail, Ernest Walker insisted that I reconsider trying out for the talent show. He would not take "no" for an answer. He proceeded to come by my house every single day for the next two weeks trying to talk me into participating. This is no exaggeration. His persistence was unrelenting. From day one through day thirteen of his daily trips to my home, I remained resistant to his demands. However, with each day, my reluctancy was fading. Unbeknownst to me, day fourteen would be the day I would crack under Ernest Walker's pressure. This day, he challenged my manhood. He said, "Fred, man, I need you to be in this talent show with me. I need you to stop acting like a little ole punk"! Maybe it was the word punk or maybe it was the tone of his voice. On the other hand, maybe it was just the fact that deep down inside, I really wanted to be in the talent show. Before I could stop myself, I said, "Punk? I ain't nobody's punk! I'll do it"! When those three words "I'll do it" came out of my mouth, I was devastated! I couldn't believe that

I had just committed to performing on stage in front of a group of people. I literally felt like passing out. On the other hand, Earnest was jumping with joy. He could not contain himself. He said, "Man you gonna do it for real"? In my frustration, I replied, "Yea, I said I'm gonna do it. Now get out of here before I change my mind"! When Ernest left, I sat in my room quietly, in deep thought. I began to replay past failures in my mind and visualized the worst thing that could happen. Unconsciously, I was trying to talk myself out of it. However, my word was my bond. I always keep promises that I make. Instead of talking myself out of the show, I started talking myself into it. I kept telling myself, "*I can do this. I am prepared for this. I am built for this. I'll block out all of the naysayers. I can perform in front of a crowd. I want to be a rap star. I want to be a DJ. I can do it*"!

Feeling invigorated and with a new sense of purpose, I knew I had to do this. I realized that I needed to give all of those bullies from my childhood a reason to know my name. I had to give them a reason to respect me. Therefore, I made a shift in my life. I started writing my own raps with my own original style. There were no more Run DMC re-writes. The shift would serve as one of the most important keys to success for me later in life. It is ok to follow someone else's lead when getting started. However, there will come a time when you have to construct your own unique style to reach a higher level. I began to practice more than ever before. Incessantly, I practiced alone in front of my mirror striving for perfection. Finally, the day for our performance arrived. It was only the first-level tryouts and I was so nervous. There were just about twenty people in the audience, which included the judges and other students trying out for the show. However, that did not matter. I was still scared out of my wits. It felt like there were twenty thousand people looking directly at me instead of twenty people. As my name was called, I took a deep breath and waited for the music track to begin. It felt like an eternity before the music started. However, it was really only a few seconds. Once the music started, in a strong voice I belted out "Call me Mr. Chill or don't call me at all. Cause when

I'm on the mic, I'm standing tall. I'm 5 foot 4, when I'm talking to you, but when I'm on the mic, I'm 7-2"! Those are the exact lyrics I spoke back then as a bashful kid with stage fright beyond measure. From the moment I spoke that first word, my life was changed. I felt an indescribable joy, peace and exuberance. I perfectly nailed my rap lyrics in the correct cadence and tone. I felt like I was on top of the world. In that moment, I thought, *this is what I was called to do*. After that, my shyness was forever released. Confidence filled the spaces that shyness once occupied. Instantly, I developed personality and character. The next day at school, it seemed like everyone knew my name.

A brand new world opened up for me that day because someone else believed in me more than I believed in myself. When I finally took that step outside of my comfort zone, the intimidating factors of fear and shyness were no longer present. Hip-hop not only helped me break those strongholds, but it also became my safe place. I was able to use hip-hop as a therapeutic measure to release frustrations. Whenever I had an issue or problem that I did not know how manage, I would simply put my pen to pad and write about the situation in a rap. To effectively manage the stressors of life, we all need to release that energy in a positive manner.

I initially channeled the release of stress through sports and then evolved to writing hip-hop lyrics. People often utilize negative releases when they do not know what their positive releases are. I implore you to figure how you can release any bottled up frustration, emotions or problems in a way that is productive and positive. That release may come in the form of sports, writing, drawing, speaking, dancing or singing to name a few. Positive releases help to protect your physical and mental health! I was virtually a nobody; a shy, bullied, fearful kid from North Tulsa who felt powerless. Little did I know that after the talent show, my life would never be the same. That is why I always say, "Hip-hop saved my life"!

CHAPTER

5

(From DC BOYS to Playya 1000)

"Victory again Freddy Boy and D Chill"
"If you know these guys you're true to the heart real"
"From D.C. B.O.Y.S to Playya 1 Gee and Deeksta"
"This song is for our true fans, pleasure to meet ya"
Lyrics taken from verse 2 of
Playya 1000 and The Deeksta's song "25 Years"
(Full song available on all streaming platforms)

The talent show took place during my ninth grade year and I was attending Tulsa McLain High School. Although there were no awards given to those who participated in the talent show, my performance was regarded as one of the best. The rap performance essentially put me on the map at Tulsa McLain High School. Home of the Mighty Scots, Tulsa McLain was one of the lowest performing schools in the state of Oklahoma. In the midst of my newfound popularity, I knew that McLain High School was less than desired because of its notoriety. Before enrolling in the school, I must admit that I was very worried about attending there. There were many awful stories floating around in the community about upperclassmen bullying incoming freshman. Having prior experiences with being bullied, those stories created much tension and anxiety within me. Luckily, I was held in high esteem and was able to circumvent things of that nature. Once, again, I was saved by hip-hop.

Initially, I did not realize the impact of my rap performance at school. Prior to the talent show, I was virtually invisible. Very few classmates acknowledged me or even knew who I was for that matter. After the performance, my student life changed considerably. In the blink of an eye, I was on everyone's radar. This was a school with nearly five hundred students and it seemed like everyone knew me. Other students who I did not know were deliberately vying for my time and attention. Not only was I not bullied by the upperclassmen, they actually became quite protective of me. I was well-liked and highly respected. No one ever gave me any problems. McLain was a school that could be very difficult to navigate because of its reputation. Luckily, my talent show performance catapulted me beyond reproach. It seemed like I was untouchable. Once again, hip-hop had placed me in a powerful position.

Although I was a sports fanatic, I became more enthusiastic about music after the talent show. It became my top priority. By my sophomore year, sports had taken a back-seat to my music ambitions. Lunch room rap sessions at school became a regular occurrence. Random students would ask me to rap while someone else beat-boxed. Those were very joyous times at McLain High School. Simultaneously, I was preparing for my dream of becoming a rap star. Hip-hop had infiltrated my mind, body and soul. It was all I thought about. I was always writing new rhymes, developing new beats and becoming better at what I thought was my destiny.

I once used hip-hop to write an essay. My high school hosted an essay contest in which participating students were required to write a letter to the next President of the United States. It was an election year and George H. Bush was campaigning for President that year. Boasting a five hundred dollar reward to the winner, the essay contest became extremely enticing. Back then, winning that kind of money was like winning ten-thousand dollars, especially where I come from. I really wanted to win that money. I imagined how those proceeds could jumpstart my rap career. Thus, I decided to enter the essay contest. Instead of writing the essay in typical fashion, I wrote it as a rap. Every two lines of the essay rhymed. Therefore, it had a rhythmic flow. There was enormous chatter and buzz amongst the teachers about my essay. They were especially impressed by the manner in which I constructed my essay as well as its content. Various teachers gave commendations about the originality and creativity of the essay.

Many students began calling me Michael Jackson because I was musically talented and had already won a plethora of awards at school. I was one of the top students in my class, ultimately graduating at number four. I had swept nearly all of the major awards given at the school. Winning became so common that I was somewhat embarrassed about entering the essay contest. However, I secretly hoped that the outcome would be no different from the other previous contests I had entered. I wanted so badly to win the contest and the money. The essay contest was eventually narrowed down to five finalists and I was among them. As the teacher walked to the podium the day of the awards ceremony, I was praying to be announced as the winner. It seemed like she was walking on the stage in slow motion. My heart was pounding and my palms were sweaty. It felt like it took her an hour to reach the podium to announce the winner. When she finally reached the podium, I took a deep breath and held it. She leaned towards the microphone and excitedly announced, "The winner is Fred Frierson." I exhaled a sigh of relief. With slight embarrassment, I cheerfully accepted the award. This was another moment of using hip-hop as a platform and reaping the reward in front of my peers. I must say, it was an awesome experience. I was a teenager feeling grateful, excited and unstoppable.

Hip-hop was still in its infancy stage and many artists were developing their own sound and style that separated them from other rappers. Like most underground rappers, I was a solo act. I was in the process of perfecting my own sound and style of rapping. My friend, Ernest Walker knew that I was trying to reach a higher level in the hip-hop game so he introduced me to a guy named Kerry Jackson. This meeting was a divine moment of my rap career. Kerry was an excellent beatboxer. His sound was much like that of Doug E. Fresh, the connoisseur of beat-boxing. Doug E. Fresh is highly revered in hip-hop and is commonly referred to as the "The Original Human Beat Box." Unbelievably, he was able to imitate special effects and drum machines in a masterful way. Soon after meeting Kerry, he introduced me to another lyrical rap artist that everyone called "Snoop." His rapping style was distinctly different from mine, which lent a nice variety to our sound. Thereafter, Snoop introduced me to a guy named Darrell Davis, who is still my best friend to this day. Darrell was a disc jockey or "DJ." Lastly, I was introduced to a guy named Goodeau who was a beat-boxer like Kerry. However, Goodeau's sound was more of a heavy bass beatboxer similar to the Human Beat Box of the group Fat Boys. We all attended Tulsa McLain High School.

One day, we all agreed to meet and practice our music in my garage and thus, our rap group was created. Since I had been a solo act prior to forming the group, I thought I was a "jack of all trades." I figured I would do a bit of everything, from deejaying, rapping and a little beatboxing. However, as the roles of our group became clearer, I quickly learned that my strength was rapping. Other members of the group were much better at deejaying and beatboxing. I was completely in awe of Darrell and his deejaying skills. One day he came to my house with an old, raggedy turntable. I connected it to the sound system and tested it out with my deejay expertise. Afterwards, Darrell showed me his skills on the turntable. My jaw dropped as he scratched the record on the turntable like he was Jam Master Jay himself. At that moment, I knew that Darrell was clearly the group's deejay. I gracefully bowed out of the notion of doing any type of deejay activities. The lesson from this example is to make sure you fully understand your unique craft. Stay in your lane and operate in your God given gift, not someone else's! That day, we all knew that Snoop and I would be the rappers of the group. Kerry, whom we called "Kerry J," was our sound beatboxer, Goodeau was our bass beatboxer, and of course, Darrell was our deejay. Now that our group was formed, all we needed was a name.

Def Chill boys or "DC Boys" for short became the name of our new rap group. Over the course of time, we would change the meaning of DC Boys, but "Def Chill Boys" was the original. We quickly began competing against other aspiring rap groups in our area. We started out performing at local school talent shows. Also, every Friday we would battle rap against other groups after football games. Most of the time, we emerged victorious. We were swiftly making a name for ourselves in our home area. I was riding high on the success and wanted to do even more. I remember sitting at home one day listening to music. I wondered how groups like Run DMC and solo artists like LL Cool J got their big break. Suddenly, it occurred to me to see if there were any recording studios in my home area. To my relief, there were.

After researching the phone book, I located a recording studio in Skiatook, Oklahoma, a small town about twenty miles north of Tulsa. I called the studio and scheduled a recording session. I was beyond excited! I could not believe that we were actually going to record a song. In preparation, we perfected our rhymes hoping to separate ourselves from competitors. On the day of our session, we recorded our first song called "Run It Back." We were all elated! We just knew it would be our first hit. Feeling hyped and full of energy after the recording session, we decided to walk home rather than call for a ride. We grabbed our equipment and began the trek home. All the while, we happily talked about the recording session and anticipated hit rap song. All was well with the exception of one issue. We had not considered the area from which we were walking. Skiatook was mostly comprised of people who didn't see us as their equals. They drove past us and stared with looks of disgust on their faces. What happened next was the harsh reality of the deep-seeded act of racism. A group of white men in a red pick-up truck slowed down to a crawl as they were passing us. They rolled down their window, leaned out, and yelled loudly "Look how black they are"! That incident reminded us that racism is real and senseless. For safety, we immediately turned around and ran back to the studio. Once we arrived back at the studio, we called Darrell's mother who picked us up. This was one of the few times in my life that I experienced real racism. That situation killed my vibe that day, but not my passion for rap music.

After recording that first song, our group was gaining more local traction and getting busier with performances. Unfortunately, Goodeau's parents forced him to leave the group because of our busy schedule. When Goodeau departed, we were left with four members of the DC Boys. This included myself, known as "Freddy Boy"; Darrell, known as "D-Chill"; Snoop, known as "Snoopy Boy"; and Kerry, known as "Kerry J." Snoop and Kerry were a year older than Darrell and I. During my senior year, since Snoop and Kerry were no longer in high school, they were not allowed to perform in school related functions with us like talent shows or pep rallys. Darrell and I were often left to perform as a duo in those situations. Although our group maintained a close friendship bond, we were unable to have regular group practices in my garage as before. Being that Snoop and Kerry were older, their way of life had changed, as it often does after graduation from high school.

Although Kerry and Snoop's attendance at group practices were sporadic, we still considered ourselves a group. Back then, I could never imagine myself not being a part of the DC Boys. Thus, Darrell and I continued to work hard in getting the right break in the rap industry. There was a local radio station in North Tulsa called KBLK. To our advantage, I had previously established a relationship with the owner of the radio station. Even though the station did not play much hip-hop music, they really liked the DC Boys. In efforts to appeal to hip-hop listeners, the owner decided to create a Saturday morning show called the Def Chill Hour. It was a great honor to have a radio show named after our group. The host of the show, "Jimmy J" became a great friend of ours. The DC Boys were featured on the show on regular basis. Through that radio show, we established a following of our music in the community. More people became familiar with us and our music. The radio station owner liked us so much that Darrell and I were ultimately hired as deejays. We would sneak our songs in during our sets and play them as much as possible. This helped the DC Boys to gain even more popularity. Our group won innumerable talent shows, performed with national recording artists and we are all still good friends to this day.

Back when the DC Boys were still trying to achieve national recognition, I met Leo Okeke, a music super producer from Boston. He had worked with big name groups like New Edition and New Kids on the Block. Leo showed interest in our work and extended an invitation to record a few songs at his local studio. *Do I Really Care* was a song recorded by the DC Boys in Leo's studio. It gained widespread popularity within our home community. After Leo, we met Randy Hammontree who was the owner of a studio called Studio 10. Randy's studio was filled with all the latest equipment and technology. He was a seasoned producer in the music industry and I sought to learn everything from him that I could. Randy took me under his wing and showed me how to run a studio. Actually, he hired me as an engineer and gave me access to free studio time. This blessing allowed the freedom to create more music on the best recording devices. It was at Studio 10 that the most popular DC Boys song was recorded called *Do I Deserve You?* When that song was released, we just knew that we were headed for fame and fortune. However, we didn't have the necessary resources in place and thus, we were unable to capitalize on the buzz that was created from the song. Darrell and I were the primary producers of DC Boys music and since Darrell did not rap, I found myself as the only voice on many of our songs.

As time passed, the attendance of Kerry and Snoop at recording sessions was becoming less and less. Being that their presence was dwindling, I decided to make a name for myself as a solo artist. However, I did not want to abandon the DC Boys brand. I made a conscious effort to continue supporting my group while establishing myself as a solo artist. What I did next was a win-win for myself as a solo artist and for our group. At that time, I had been collaborating with a local group called Small Town Playyas. I was an honorary member of the group. My stage name with that group was Playya 1000 (one-thousand). In contrast, my stage name within the DC Boys group was "Freddy Boy." There were a few songs that I had written for the DC Boys that had not been recorded. I decided to record those songs under the stage name Playya 1000. From that decision, Playya 1000 was born as a solo artist. Darrell or "D-Chill," our deejay from the DC boys became a silent member of my solo act of Playya 1000. With Playya 1000, Darrell's stage name was "The Deeksta." He was mostly responsible for helping with the music production. In the first Playya 1000 release, I gave a "shout-out" to Freddy Boy as if he and I were not the same person. Doing that was my attempt to keep the peace between the two groups. I wanted to ensure Darrell, Kerry and Snoop that I was still very much a part of the DC Boys. However, I had also found a new energy and artistry through the solo act of Playya 1000. I am still widely known by that stage name today.

The first album I released under the Playya 1000 stage name was called "Reality." In my determination to release this album, the owner of studio 10, Randy Hammontree taught me how to create professional cassettes. I was working with a very small income and needed to establish an efficient and economical way to release my music. Randy was an invaluable part of that process. He taught me what he knew. This included distribution to local stores. In time, I had a local hit under the name Playya 1000. I had also earned enough money to keep making music, this time a bit more seriously. By the time that I was distributing my own Playya 1000 music, the DC Boys had officially disbanded. However, Darrell and I continued to work together on various music projects. Now our official stage name was Playya 1000 and the The Deeksta. The next album we released was called "Blame it on Society." Prior to this album, our music had always been released on cassette tapes. This time, we were releasing our music on CDs as well. Using an entrepreneurial mindset along with the determination of gaining a national following, I developed a game plan to grow our music. In hip-hop magazines, I noticed that mom-and-pop record stores across the nation were frequently mentioned. I used that information to compile a contact list of small record stores. Thereafter, I would send each of the stores our album for a listening review. I was hoping that sending our music to these mom and pop music stores would drastically improve our reach to hip-hop listeners beyond the state of Oklahoma. And, it did! Our music was sent to places such as Louisville, Seattle, Denver, Omaha, and many others. Our music would be played in various stores and the customers loved it. The stores would immediately contact me to place orders for more CDs. My company was called Federal Entertainment and I was selling CDs cash on delivery, which was a very good business at that time. I was able to make a decent living and noticed that our music was gaining national traction.

From the overwhelming response to our music, I received a call from Select-O-Hits, a music distribution company based out of Memphis, Tennessee. They wanted to distribute our "Blame it on Society" album. I am not sure how they became aware of the album, but I suspect it was through Disc Makers, the company that originally pressed our album. Disc Makers was a national cassette and CD pressing company. They asked us to give a testimonial of how well they had done on our project. We gladly provided the testimonial as they requested. To our surprise, the testimonial and our album cover was placed on their marketing pamphlets and distributed nationwide. This provided us with credibility in the music game and because of that; Select- O-Hits contacted us. The distribution company was home to several highly successful national hip-hop recording artists. As you can imagine, I was super-excited about Select-O-Hits wanting to distribute our album. We were given a couple of options in working with Select-O-Hits. We could either agree to a pressing and distribution deal, called a "P & D" or sign directly to their record label. If we chose to sign directly to their label, Select-O-Hits would press and distribute our albums while also handling promotion and marketing. I was becoming more entrepreneurial minded during this time. In addition, I had my own successful distribution company, Federal Entertainment. Because of this, I was not willing to relinquish control over my music. Consequently, We chose the "P & D" deal. Choosing the "P & D" deal allowed Federal Entertainment to maintain the previously established distribution relationships with mom and pop stores while Select-O-Hits focused on national music store chains. The deal also allowed Darrell and I to continue our own marketing and branding.

Once we released the "Blame it on Society" album, I was selling out the units at a fast pace. The folks at Select-O-Hits were stunned that I kept requesting additional units. They asked how I was able to sell so many units in such a short time-span. I explained that one of my strengths is building relationships. I would intentionally develop a strong relationship with the mom and pop record stores by sending them a promotional copy of our CD and also through phone conversations. I knew that record stores on the receiving end of a promo CD would be more likely to listen to it and play the music for their patrons. In turn, if their customers enjoyed the music, the record store would contact me to purchase copies of the album that I would sell at a discounted rate. I knew that for independent stores, it was in their best interest to give underground music an opportunity because it was through these artists that they typically profited. The distribution process supported the development of our next project, the "Mo Drama" album. Little did we know that a song from this project would become the most popular song ever recorded by Playya 1000 and the Deeksta.

Sunday Afternoon was the title of the song on the "Mo Drama" album that took Tulsa by storm. This song was a tribute to the carefree, fun times in North Tulsa that we had every

Sunday "back in the day." People in the community would dress up in the latest gear and meet at a burger joint called Tastee Freeze. We would all gather there around four o'clock in the evening every Sunday. The ladies would often show off their new clothing, hairstyles and meet up with their click of friends. The guys would have their clean haircuts, show off the latest athletic tennis shoes and meet up with their friends as well. We had fun socializing, dancing, listening to music and eating one those heavenly burgers from Tastee Freeze. There was also a popular car wash adjacent to Tastee Freeze. Everyone would be washing their cars making sure that their rides and rims were fresh and clean. Some even drove their motorcycles. It was a sight to see. There would be hundreds of people hanging out and having fun. Before darkness set in, everyone would leave Tastee Freeze and head to our favorite hangout spot in North Tulsa, O'Brien Park. Having specific, hangout areas was not just a local thing. Actually, people all across America in various cities have their favorite hangout locations where they celebrate and socialize. In the song, "Sunday Afternoon," Darrell and I were able to capture the essence of not only enjoying life while hanging out at our city's favorite spot , but we were also able to capture the essence of how others felt while hanging out at their city's favorite spot as well!

At the time, we had no idea of the impact that *Sunday Afternoon* would have on people nationally and internationally. However, I remember that during the process of recording the "Mo Drama" album, Tim Dobbins, a local rap artist came into the studio as Darrell and I were finishing a session. We took a minute to let Tim hear a few songs from the "Mo' Drama" project. When we played *Sunday Afternoon*, about mid-way through the song, Tim held up his hand signifying for us to stop the track. He then intentionally pointed to the speaker and emphatically stated, "That's it. That's the one"! When he said that, we knew that we had something special. We just didn't know how special. Since then, that song has taken us to places we could never have imagined. It was, and has been a bigger hit than we ever dreamed. More units of the "Mo' Drama" project were sold than we ever anticipated.

We gained instant success and that song remains one of the most popular underground hip-hop songs to this day. At that time, we thought we were well on our way to stardom.

Playya 1000 & the Deeksta nearly always received kudos and much love from hometown fans. But sadly, there were also instances of jealousy and hate. For the thousands of people who supported our music, there was always one person whose sole mission was to knock us down. The story I am going to share is unthinkable, but true. To this day, it is still hard for me to fathom that it really happened. As I stated earlier, I have always worked hard at building relationships and adding value to others. Therefore, I made a concerted effort to visit our local radio station at least monthly to keep the Playya 1000 & the Deeksta brand on their radar. Additionally, I continued to cultivate a positive relationship with the program director. This was particularly important because the program director determines what songs are played on the air. After arriving at the radio station during my monthly visit, I went to the program director's office. As I entered the room, he looked up at me as if he had seen a ghost. An expression of concern was all over his face. He seemed very uncomfortable and I immediately knew something was wrong. His greeting was very different from our normal handshake, hug, and smile. Although I sensed something wasn't right, I acknowledged him with my normal greeting of "How's everything going"? In response, he said, "No bro, the question is, how is everything going with you"? Based on his response, I knew something was definitely wrong, but in efforts to gauge the situation, I simply stated, "I'm great"!

Normally, our conversations were filled with smiles, cordial chatter and a friendly tone, but this encounter was the exact opposite. He gazed intently at me, paused, and then finally said in a stuttering voice "Hey, did you send me a letter"? I quickly replied, "No, I have not sent you a letter. What do you mean"? After that, he sternly said, "follow me." I slowly followed him into another room. I had no idea what was going on or what was about to happen. All I knew was something was seriously wrong. This was not his normal demeanor and it felt extremely uncomfortable. Upon entering the back room, he opened a file cabinet and pulled out a letter. He handed me the folded letter and said, "Are you sure that you did not send me this letter"? I reiterated, "No sir! Why would I send you a letter, unless it was a gift"? He then instructed me to read the letter. I opened the letter and proceeded to read it aloud. What I read was just as shocking to me as it was to him. The content of the letter thoroughly explained his reactions when he saw me. The letter was sent to him from someone pretending to be me. We haven't ever been able to ascertain the responsible person. This is what was written in the letter:

To whom it may concern:

This is Playya 1000. I am requesting that you stop playing my music effective immediately. I have contracted the HIV virus and will be forced to retire from music.

At that point, I stopped reading the letter, looked directly at the program director and just busted out laughing. To me, it was comical. I wondered who would actually take time to write such a letter, put a stamp on it and mail it. It reminded me of how poisonous envy can be. After gathering myself from laughing so hard, I said to the program director, "Bro, I did not send you that letter. And, for the record, I am fine." There was a huge look of relief on his face. He said "Thank goodness! I have felt so bad for you since I received that letter." That letter was very disturbing. It was a harsh reality of how conniving some people can be. No matter how well things are going in your life, there will always be people who want to see you fail. That letter was sent to inflict harm. So, whenever I feel like giving up or not pushing through, I always think back to that letter. I changed my perception about it and now it serves as the fuel that drives me to continue doing my best. From the day I read that letter, I made a vow to never let the hater that wrote it see me fail. If hate like that ever comes your way, make sure you use it as fuel to keep grinding harder and harder on your journey to greatness! Do not ever allow anyone or anything to deter you in achieving your mission of success!

Shortly after I received that letter of hate, hip-hop went mainstream. That change created a critical transformation in the sound of hip-hop because the purity was removed from the music. Previously, major record labels shied from the art form because they believed hip-hop was a passing fad. To their surprise, hip-hop surged into a global success. Thereafter, record companies began signing new hip-hop artists and releasing music at an alarming rate. I previously hoped that hip-hop would never go mainstream. Because I knew, if the major record labels took over, it would be difficult for underground artists to compete. Once hip-hop went mainstream, the market became saturated with artists. Money began to rule the industry. It became more difficult to have promo CDs played in the mom and pop stores. The major record labels began paying the smaller record stores to play the music of their mainstream artists. That marked the end of success for most independent labels, such as Federal Entertainment. All of sudden, radio play was needed to market music to the masses. Video play was also needed in addition to handsome budgets for promotion. Most independent artists were not able to compete on this level. The change of hip-hop going mainstream significantly reduced the sales of Federal Entertainment. When our next album was released, the sales were not great. People preferred to hear a song repeatedly on the radio before deciding if they wanted to buy. That eliminated any momentum we might have had in selling our music. Concurrently, some personal life changes caused the music of Playya 1000 and The Deeksta to be halted for an extended period.

CHAPTER

(Young and Reckless)

"Imperfect person, but perfect resembles no man"
"Misguided steps as a youth, guess it was God's plan"
"Precautions never took, broke really had no sense"
"I'm talking money or common, ignorance in a sense"
Lyrics taken from verse 1 of
Playya 1000 and The Deeksta's song "So Simple"
(Full song available on all streaming platforms)

While gaining local and regional hip-hop fame, in many ways I was a hot mess. I was young and reckless. I did whatever felt good in the moment. Although I was on the verge of achieving my dream of becoming a hip-hop superstar, irresponsibility plagued my life. I was far from being a thug, but my general mindset was careless and impulsive. In contrast, I functioned quite well within my strength of creating, producing and distributing music. Thus, my entrepreneurial prowess led me to become more successful than other aspiring rap artists in my community. Yet, outside of the realm of music, I lacked focus and direction.

Having no sense of direction became apparent in my senior year of high school. I was walking the halls during my yearbook elective class, as I often did. I saw a young lady in the hallways who had just dropped her schoolbooks. I went over to help her pick up the books when she curtly said "Back off! I don't know you! I'll pick up my own books"! She was very sassy and cute. She had much attitude, which in my mind made her even prettier. We eventually began a relationship. A few years later, she became pregnant and we had our first child. I was broke and desperate to find a way to provide for my child. It was a difficult time being that I didn't have a regular, steady job. To make matters worse, my baby's mother lived in "the projects" while I still lived at home with my parents. There was frequent crime and drug activity in the apartments where my girlfriend lived. Drug dealers regularly sold crack cocaine there. Although I was not involved in any type of drug activity, many of the people who sold drugs were my closest friends.

One day, a guy living in those same projects cautiously approached me about helping him become involved in selling drugs. He wanted to get into the drug game to make quick, easy money. We knew each other relatively well and he knew that it was not in my character to become involved with drugs. However, he was also aware that some of the major drug dealers in the area were some of my closest friends. Another thing that he knew is that I had a baby that I needed to support. With some resistance, he asked if I would be willing to play the "go-between" or middleman in selling crack cocaine. He knew that the major drug dealers would never deal directly with him. Thus, he used my current situation as a means of gaining help with his goal of becoming a drug dealer. He explained that in being the middleman, I would obtain the crack cocaine from my source and, in turn, provide him with the drugs. He would then take the drugs and sell them on the streets. After selling the drugs, he would provide me with my requested cut of the money. From my proceeds, I would pay the "plug," also known as the supplier while making sure that there was plenty left over for myself.

Being that some of the major drug dealers were my closet friends, they knew that I had no desire to become involved in the drug game. They had much respect for me and never tried to entice me to get involved in the game. Hence, I knew they would be shocked if I ever approached them about taking part in the drug game. Yet, I also knew that they would oblige me if I ever asked. I remembered that I had vowed to never become involved with drugs. However, by this time, I felt I had no other recourse. I was young and desperate to provide for my child. I had lost all reasoning and morals. The drug game proposition was very tempting and I knew that it was also very dangerous. I was nervous and afraid about giving any thought to dealing drugs, but I needed quick money. I had earned some proceeds from selling music, but that was not enough. I toiled with the idea of dealing drugs. I kept telling myself to resist any involvement; that I did not need to resort to drug dealing for money. After much angst and against my better judgment, I reluctantly became the middleman in dealing crack cocaine. By then, I was so mentally lost and broken. I had lost all sense of who I really was. Internally, I was in shambles. Externally, I kept up the façade that I was "living my best life." In actuality, it was the worst life that I could have imagined for myself. I remember writing lyrics in a rap verse that captured my feelings:

> In shock, I stop and I wonder. Said I'd never do it, but I blew it, cause the hood done took me under. So never say never, you never know, cause you just my say f**k it and like go with the flow."

Honestly, I did not know what else to do. My juvenile ways and immaturity opened the door to a perilous lifestyle. Truth be told, I was scared to death. Frankly, I did not want to be a dope man. I never smoked, never drank, never joined a gang, but my life was in total disarray. I was ruining my clean-cut reputation and chances of having a rap career.

By this time, the local police knew about the drug activities going on in the apartment complex. To remain unsuspecting, police officers often dressed in plain clothes. Some of them were undercover cops posing as dope fiends. Some were cops in uniform targeting groups of guys hanging out in the projects. They would often rush groups with their bright lights at nighttime. Many of the guys were quick on their feet and could not be caught. Others were slow and easily accosted by the police.

Other than when I initially arrived at the projects, I rarely had any drugs on me. Nevertheless, if someone else ran, I ran too. Many times, I would have no idea why we were running other than thinking that the police were coming. Usually, if police were chasing us, we would have specific hiding places or apartments that we ran to for safety. Most of the time, the cops were not able to find us. Like everyone else, I would hide patiently while waiting for the cops to leave. One particular day, my patience wore off too quickly and I came out of hiding too soon. As soon as I walked around the corner of the building, there were two cops sitting in their car looking directly at me. Instantly, we made eye contact. My heart dropped to my feet. I was totally caught off guard. I did not expect to see the cops sitting there. I just knew that this was the day that I would be taken to jail. I figured the drug game had finally caught up with me. The cops motioned for me to come to their car. I knew I could not out run them this time so I slowly walked toward their vehicle. I will never forget what one of the police officers said. His words were "Your name is Fred, ain't it? Word on the street is that you're in a group called the DC Boys and that you're out here selling crack cocaine to get money for studio time." My mouth dropped open so wide. I thought, *how could he have known that information?* I was in total shock. I knew that there was no possible way he could have known that information without someone in my circle ratting me out. I didn't have any drugs on me at the time so I didn't go to jail that day, but I learned a valuable lesson: There is no honor amongst thieves. Problem was, even though I knew that someone close to me was feeding information to the police, it did not deter me from continuing with drug dealing.

At that point in time, I had not actually sold any drugs directly to users. I was still the middleman in the drug transactions, but that quickly escalated. A little while thereafter, I learned that the guy who had propositioned me about getting into the drug game was actually using the supply I would give to him to sell. In essence, he was not only the dealer, but he had also become a user. I knew something wasn't right when my profits began dwindling. His new drug habit resulted in him cutting into my profits. I had become comfortable with having money and plenty of it. Even though I was terrified to sell the crack cocaine myself, I was not ready to give up the easy money generated from being the middleman. Since my seller had become a crack addict himself, I had to make some decisions about my involvement. Once again, I caved in and chose to continue operating in the drug game. With regret, I personally started selling drugs directly to the crack addicts. I was officially no longer the middle man. I was now directly in the line of fire.

One day, my kid's mom and I were visiting her friend who lived in a different set of projects. Her friend's boyfriend also dealt drugs. At the time of our visit, we were told that the area was "hot." That meant that cops were raiding specific areas of the apartment complex. We were advised to stay away to avoid any police officers. My baby's mom remained at the apartment with her friend. The boyfriend and I left the area and went to my dad's house. We hung out there for a while to allow things to die down then headed back to the apartments. As we were returning, we thought we saw police cars in front of his apartment. Immediately, our hearts dropped. We thought the cops were waiting for us. Instead of driving into the complex, we circled the corner to get a better look at what was happening around the apartment. When we came back, we didn't see any police cars. We thought we were in the clear. As it turns out, we were not in the clear. My baby's mom and her friend were both taken to jail. We were devastated! We didn't think that would ever happen. In the drug game, there were rumors that cops wouldn't search a female. As a result, drugs would often be put on the person of a female because it was thought that only males would be searched. Turns out, that was not the case. Female cops were used to search suspects of

45

the same sex. This is what caused my kid's mom to be taken to jail. When the cops raided the apartment, she put all of the drugs on her person. Some of the drugs belonged to me and some belonged to her friend's boyfriend.

Although the cops knew that my baby's mom was not the actual drug dealer, she was booked into jail and hit with multiple drug charges. However, she caught a break. Her friend told the police that all of the drugs belonged to her boyfriend. Ultimately, all of the drug charges were placed against the boyfriend and he ended up serving several years in the penitentiary for those drug charges. All charges were dropped against my baby's mother and somehow there was never any discussion about me being involved with the drugs or even being present at the apartment. I know that my baby's mom played a pivotal role in keeping me from being placed behind bars. For that, I am eternally grateful. I feel like this was also a moment of favor and protection provided by my guardian angel, my mother. I do not have any other way of explaining it. It was one of the biggest blessings of my life and a turning point for me.

From that day on, I vowed never to sell drugs again. I matured a bit and began to view life differently. Even so, I was still living foul and reckless. By the time I was twenty-five years old, we had four kids together. There were three girls and one boy, but we were no longer in a relationship. Often, I would pick up the kids and take them to an arcade in Tulsa called the Fun House. We would do fun things like that occasionally. I had also begun dating another young lady who had five kids of her own. Still, I really was not thinking things through before acting. Here I was, twenty-five years old and driving around with nine kids in my mini-van. It was wild and thoughtless. To worsen matters, I had all sorts of issues aside from the person I was dating. I was very irresponsible when it came to operating and maintaining my vehicle. I had no means of paying for car insurance so I drove around uninsured. Frequently, I would be stopped by the police for swerving all over the road. This would happen primarily at night. The problem was that I could not see clearly while driving. I was supposed to wear glasses, but they made me look nerdy. Because I wanted to look cool, I chose not to wear my glasses. I was pulled over frequently for this very problem and each time I was given a traffic ticket. I often neglected to pay the traffic tickets so my fines and fees were astronomical. Due to non-payment of traffic tickets, my driver's license was suspended and I had warrants out for my arrest. Nonchalantly, I ignored all of these things. I kept driving under suspension, with warrants and reduced vision. Every time I was pulled over by a police officer, I was digging a deeper hole for myself and I had absolutely no clue.

I continued to ignore the rules of life. I was totally out of control and was desperately in need of help. One night, Darrell, Snoop, and I were going to a football game. It was a rivalry game between Tulsa McLain and Tulsa Washington. Everyone we knew was going to be there so we were excited about going. We were driving to the game when we were pulled over by the cops. Darrell was driving. Not only did he ask for Darrell's license, but Snoop's license was requested as well as mine. I became very nervous because I knew there was a good change that a warrant had been issued for my arrest. However, I tried to keep my cool and not let the fellas see me sweat. When the officer came back to car, he asked me to step out of the car. He said the words I was praying not to hear: "You have a warrant out for your arrest." I was devastated! I was taken to jail that night. I tried everything I knew to avoid being arrested. I went through the theatrics of crying, panting, and whining to no avail. Darrell and Snoop thought it was the funniest thing ever and they still tease me about it to this day. This was a crazy, rough patch in my life but, believe it or not, the silliness continued.

I once had an opportunity to work at a modern rock station as a guest DJ for a guy that had a hip-hop show. While at the station, I would go through the different rooms during my down time just checking out their music. Back then, I frequently sampled music from other artists when creating new songs. I would try to find the most obscure rhythm and blues records to sample cool beats. One of the rooms just happened to have a boatload of classic R&B albums in it. I thought to myself, *this is a modern rock station. Surely, they won't miss a few R&B records, right?* Slowly, I began taking R&B records from the station. Nobody seemed to notice at first. Week after week, I would take a few records at a time. I eventually compiled a stack of the records to use for developing my own songs. I thought that no one would ever notice that the records were missing. That was until one day, another DJ asked me about some of the missing records, but I denied having any knowledge about them. My lies didn't work. The station owner quickly figured out that I had taken the records. In an effort to cover my tracks, I moved the records to Darrell's house just in case the police searched my home. The station owner eventually called the police and reported me. However, I was tipped off that they were heading to my house. Just as I was about to leave, they had already arrived as I was coming up to my front door. I panicked and climbed into the attic and hid there. It was winter, so it was freezing outside and in the attic. I did not have time to grab a coat so there I was, lying in my daddy's attic shivering and feeling like I was going to freeze to death. I prayed that the police would not kick in my front door and search the house. Thank goodness, they did not. Once again, I feel like my mom reached down and touched the situation and kept me out harm's way. Shortly after that episode, I called the radio station owner. I admitted my wrongdoings and agreed to give all the records back. He was still very upset with me, but agreed not to press charges. I kept my word and delivered all of the records back to the radio station.

Another time, I worked at a local record store and noticed a stack of promotional cassettes that didn't seem to be in use. The cassettes were stacked up and the pile just kept getting higher. If someone returned a cassette, whether it was defective or not, it would be put in this stack. Thinking that the cassettes were not being used, I decided to take them and sell them on the streets. I figured no one would ever miss them. Although I was never reprimanded for it, I think the store realized what I was doing. Without any warning, I was terminated shortly thereafter. They only said that my services were no longer needed. Somehow, they became aware of what I was doing. I was upset about it because a few days earlier, I had received an evaluation and scored very high, but I have nobody to blame but myself because this action was another one of my poor decisions that lacked integrity.

After I graduated from high school, I started college, but couldn't focus. College was nothing like high school where I had been able to coast by on my natural intelligence. In high school, I never studied or put any extra effort into my work. In college, the classes were much more difficult and I had to exert effort, something I was not used to doing. I just could not seem to find the motivation or proper mindset to succeed in college. I struggled greatly and eventually dropped out of college. Not too long after I had decided not pursue a college degree, a friend called me and stated, "Hey, I am up here at College of America and they're giving out free money." In my ignorance, I could not wait to benefit from that opportunity. My shortcoming was that the decision had nothing to do with school; it was all based on receiving money. What I did not realize is that the money was hardly free. College of America was giving out Pell Grants for those who qualified and it was up to the student to decide what to do with that money. As you can imagine, I did not intend to pay for school. I took the money and dropped all of my classes thereafter. This action landed me in a mountain of student loan debt. That decision had a ripple effect in destroying my credit rating. Unfortunately, I was just living life without any strategic plan or goals.

There was another time while I was driving with just my biological kids in the vehicle; the police stopped me. I do not remember why I was pulled over, but when the policeman checked my driver's license, a warrant for my arrest was found. I am sure it was for not paying some type of ticket or fine. In spite of my pleadings to avoid being arrested, the officer took me to jail in front of all of my little babies. That was one of the lowest times of my life. As I sat in that jail cell contemplating my life, I knew something had to change. Problem was, I did not know how to make the necessary changes. I was fed up with living aimlessly. I knew that there was a better version of me buried deep inside my soul. Next, I did the only thing I could think to do. I prayed and asked the Lord to guide me away from this life of strife. This was the time when things really began to change in my life for the better.

In contrast to my disastrous ways, my best friend, Darrell Davis, also known as "The Deeksta" was always grounded. Darrell and I were total opposites. He was prudent, thoughtful and he had measurable goals. Darrell was cautious in his decisions and exhibited a life of stability. Darrell knew what he wanted in life and devised a plan on how he was going to achieve his goals. He always kept a good job with benefits, and because of that, he encountered fewer struggles. Although he loves music, it has always had its proper place in his life. Unlike myself, Darrell never put music ahead of his job or ahead of himself for that matter. Even so, he was always my "ride or die" homeboy. He has always supported my ideas, even if he did not totally agree with them. He would always tell me "You need to slow your roll bro." Although we are essentially the same age, he was always like a father figure. He was full of wisdom even at a young age and most of his wise words proved right later in life. We have been best friends since high school. I regard him as a "brother from another mother." Although we are close friends, we rarely think alike and we have different personalities. I totally lived for the moment with very little regard for what might happen in the future. Darrell lived for the future with careful thought and regard for every moment. If I could relive my young, reckless years, I would more than likely follow Darrell's lead. His road was more like a smooth, peaceful ride while mine was filled with potholes and bumps all along the way. Unfortunately, I cannot change what has happened, but I did learn that I can change my future course. I am telling you my life story because I know many of you out there are much more like me, rather than Darrell. That's why I am sharing the many messes that I made in my life. Later, I will take you through the steps I took to change the error of my ways. It is my hope that this will serve as living proof that you can overcome, transform, and live a winning life of joy, internal peace and success.

CHAPTER

(The Epiphany)

"Epiphany happened call it God's work"
"Now my life is like the lotto, watch them odds work"
"In my favor cause I made the choice to transform"
"Lord had plans for him, I made through the sand storm"
Lyrics taken from verse 1 of
Playya 1000 and The Deeksta's song "Transformation"
(Full song available on all streaming platforms)

Sitting in that jail cell all alone and disenchanted with life, I hoped for better times. I knew that I couldn't continue living a fragmented existence. Spontaneously, I closed my eyes, bowed my head, put my hands together in prayer and began asking the Lord to change me. In that very moment, the seeds of change were planted by my prayer. Change did not happen overnight, however, the seeds of success were germinating inside of me. My world transformed over the coming years. I was still pursuing a rap career, but half-heartedly. It also took a while before I could maintain a regular job. I wasn't acclimated to working a nine to five job. My work ethic was horrible. There was a time when I was hired to wash cars at a local car wash company. They were extremely busy and obviously, the job required hard, manual labor. I lasted all of half a day. Yes, I did say only half a day! I left on my lunch break and never returned. I felt like I could not work a regular nine to five job because of my entrepreneurial mindset. I wanted to do other things that I felt were of more importance, like making music. Truth be told, I was just lazy. I didn't want to work. Personal growth and maturity was a necessity if I were to be successful in life. In order to achieve job stability, I knew that an adjustment in my mental perception needed to occur.

At age twenty-six, my epiphany finally arrived and it hit me like a ton of bricks. By this time, I had settled down considerably, but was still operating in some of my old ways. I was up listening to music late one evening then decided to retire for the night. I prepared for bed in my normal routine. There was nothing happening out of the ordinary and I slept well. I did not toss and turn nor did I have any bad dreams. Oddly, I woke up the next morning feeling exhilarated and almost extra-ordinary. Something was different. I remember staring at the ceiling for what seemed like an eternity. Inexplicably, I had an explicit sense of knowing; an intuition. I could clearly see all of my past failures and mistakes. The missteps in ruining my credit, incurring student loan debt and living a careless life became plainly apparent. This was far from a "woe is me" moment. It represented an unquestionable path of clarity and direction. My mindset had made a monumental shift. I somehow knew the necessary actions to take in turning my life around. Often, I say that my cerebral cortex had finally developed. The cerebral cortex is the area of the brain that controls reasoning and mine had been dormant for seemingly my entire life. Yet, my epiphany moment changed all of that. In an instant, I clearly visualized the deep hole of student loan debt, bad credit, poor work habits, traffic tickets, arrest warrants, suspended driver's license and many others. I knew that it would take a while to climb out of that deep hole, but I was not discouraged. Actually, I was eager to clean up my messes and begin that climb to the top of the massive pit I was in.

All of the thoughts that went through my head that day felt very strange. I was no longer the old me. I was a new person inside and out. My first course of action was gaining custody of my four children. They were still living with their mother, but not in the best environment. Up until that moment I never had plans to gain physical custody of the children, I would visit them periodically at their mother's house in the ghetto. Although my one bedroom apartment was not lavish by any means, I knew that my place was a safer environment for them. There was nothing spectacular about my living quarters, but I was not in the "hood." I lived in South Tulsa, which in general is a better area than North Tulsa. Furthermore, my financial state was slightly better than their mother's was. My plan was to visit with their mother about taking physical custody. Before I could make that call to her, the strangest thing happened. She actually called me and asked if I could take them for a while. When she called me, she had no idea that I had planned on speaking with her about taking physical custody. Their mother shared that she was going through rough times and needed a short break from the day-to-day responsibilities of raising four children. I happily agreed with her request.

Since my apartment had only one bedroom, I made a pallet or makeshift bed for the kids to sleep. They were elated. They helped me make the pallet out of blankets while innocently playing and enjoying their time in their new environment with me. Although the kids were super-excited, I was overwhelmed, but committed to being a full-time father. Of course, I knew that this was only a temporary arrangement. I anticipated that their mother would eventually request that they be returned to her. A week later, that is exactly what happened. Their mother called and reported that she was doing much better. She asked me to bring the kids back home to her. I agreed to take the children back to her with conditions. I explained that if she called me to take them again, I would become responsible for them on a full-time basis. That meant enrolling them in a different school in my home district and having them live with me on a permanent basis. Not believing that I was serious, she laughed, but willingly agreed.

Shortly after I returned the kids to their mother, I received a phone call from a person that knew her very well. This individual expressly stated that my children were in harm's way and that I needed to remove them from their living environment. Apparently, the man that their mother was dating was involved in illegal activities. The children were hearing and seeing these activities, which was not good. I quickly began preparing my home and mindset for the kids to live with me on a full time basis. I was done being selfish. I wanted to create a better life for my children. Unsurprisingly, their mother called me again about two weeks later. She asked if I would take the children again. Obviously, I agreed while reminding her of our agreement that I would take physical custody of the kids. Still, she was not convinced that I was serious about raising them on my own. My oldest child was seven and the youngest was three. A young, African American male single-handedly raising four children on his own was virtually unheard of where I come from. Yet, that is exactly what happened.

Immediately, I withdrew the kids from their old school and enrolled them in my home area. My youngest child was not yet in school, but the three older kids were. Funny thing, when I withdrew them from their old school, I wasn't asked to provide any type of identification proving that I was their father. The school simply processed the withdrawal at my request. I guess the school officials figured that an African-American man would not purposely claim three young kids that were not his. Anyhow, I explained my situation to them and the plan to enroll my kids in a different school. The school administrators were very excited for my kids. They had heard great things about that particular school and felt the children would do very well there. I had successfully gained physical custody of my children and literally transformed into a "Mr. Mom." My entire life was turned upside down, but I was okay with it. Life was no longer just about me. It was about my children and keeping them out of harm's way. I did my best to surround them only with positivity. This was especially important for my three older children. They had seen and heard a great deal of negativity while living in North Tulsa and I made an intentional effort to erase that from their lives. Although my living situation was not ideal, we had the basic necessities for living and the kids were overjoyed. They did not mind sleeping on a pallet in the living room. They were just happy to be there. Meanwhile, I began strategizing on ways to earn extra money (legally) and getting a bigger apartment.

The kids had been living with me full-time for about two weeks when their mother called and asked if I would bring them back home. I explained to her that I had already taken the children out of their old school and enrolled them in my school district. Naturally, she was quite surprised. Next, I had an earnest conversation with her about doing what would be in the best interest of our children. She knew that her home life needed improvement and that mine was truly the best for our children. Reluctantly, she agreed, but stated that once she was in a better living situation, she wanted the kids to come back home with her. We never went to court. There was never a custody battle or legal proceeding. Only a verbal agreement was made that we both honored. Little did I know that I would continue raising our kids full-time until they all graduated from high school and went off to college.

CHAPTER

(Survival Mode)

"And I got 4"

"They're more precious than the diamonds
that you find in a jewelry store"

"The reason why I grind is to make sure they
grow up and be the best that they can"

"So my daughters become ladies and
my son becomes a man"

Lyrics taken from verse 3 of

Playya 1000 and The Deeksta's song "Special"

(Full song available on all streaming platforms)

It was official: I was a single dad with four kids, ages three to seven. Thank goodness they were all out of diapers. Shortly after I gained custody of my children, their mother's boyfriend was murdered. Though I heard several different stories surrounding the circumstances of his death, the only thing that I am sure of is that I made the right decision to raise the kids. My children did not need to be anywhere near the types of activities that were taking place in that environment. As I was working on moving to a larger home, I realized that kids don't see struggle the same way as their parents. My kids were jumping for joy to be sleeping on a pallet in the living room while I was spazzing and stressing over our living situation. We needed more room. I felt confined, claustrophobic and I assumed they felt the same way. In reality, they had no idea we were struggling. Sometimes as parents, we are too hard on ourselves. We often unnecessarily beat ourselves down because of life's circumstances. Like myself, many parents raising small children berate themselves. Frustration, guilt and tension can derail your plans for a better life. Always remember that more than not, the children are happy. They have no clue about the stresses of life. Children do not see life through the eyes of an adult; they see life through their own innocence.

Even though I wanted physical custody of my children, it was still a major adjustment. Being a full-time single dad was exhausting at times. There was a lot I had to learn about parenting and about myself as a father. Quickly, I learned that parenting a boy is different from parenting a girl. For instance, I had to learn how to comb hair for my girls. At first, I had absolutely no idea what I was doing. Back then, there was no google search available and no YouTube videos to watch. Eventually, I came up with one hairstyle that was easy to do and that was a simple bun. Personally, I thought I had perfected it. However, as soon as my daughters were old enough to do their own hair, they quickly stopped letting me comb their hair. Honestly, I was as equally excited to allow them to take that responsibility.

After gaining custody of my kids, I realized how much time I had wasted in not designing the lifestyle I wanted to live. As a result, I was in survival mode. I knew that I would have to hustle to make ends meet, but my primary focus was ensuring my children's safety. I monitored their friends, school activities, music they listened to, and shows they watched on television. I was trying everything I could to make sure that I kept them in a positive atmosphere with positive influences. That meant putting my music dreams on hold. My life changed drastically after gaining custody of the kids. Previously, I was able to leave home at will, but that was no longer possible. Now, most of my time and attention was devoted to the children. This also meant that my music career was placed on hold. Darrell and I never specifically talked about pressing pause on our music, but he was very busy with work and I was always busy with my kids. We remained close friends throughout this phase of life, but slowly stopped making music.

I was still in the process of changing my mindset when it came to working a full-time job. It was a struggle because I did not have a trade or degree. Having only a high school degree limited the types of jobs for which I qualified. Working as a telemarketer was one those types of positions. A meager salary of nine to ten dollars an hour was common for telemarketers. That level of income was barely enough to pay the bills or daycare for that matter. I could only imagine the amount of money I would have to pay to arrange daycare for four children. I'm positive it would have been astronomical. Furthermore, I did not want to leave my children with just any babysitter. Thus, I knew that I had to find another way to earn a proper income. I concluded that a full-time job was not in my best interest at the time. Not working a full-time job meant going into hustle mode. Since I decided to be a stay-at-home dad, I reasoned that a profitable, legal side-hustle needed to be established. I desperately needed to generate enough income for food, shelter and clothing. I never asked or received any financial assistance, welfare, or food stamps from the state. In addition, I never attempted to gain child support from my kids' mother. I made a concerted decision to do everything in my power to care for my children without any assistance at all. Having made that decision opened the door for other important decisions to be made regarding income. Those decisions would need to be made quickly.

Thankfully, my drug selling days were behind me. I definitely planned not to ever go that route again. Then an idea hit me. I had previously made a decent living selling Playya 1000 and the Deeksta CDs and cassettes. However, once hip-hop went mainstream, it put a huge dent into my profits. I thought, rather than selling my own music, I would sell mixed CDs with all of the latest rap and R&B tracks. Like before, I would also distribute my CDs to different stores across the country. I switched gears and put my plan into action. I knew the types of music that most people in my neighborhood liked. I made a variety of music CDs to appeal to all. My best seller was a mixed CD entitled "Federal Jamz." It was named after my distribution company, "Federal Entertainment." I also created "Intimate Connections," which was a collection of love songs. There was also "Intimate Classics," which had all of the old school slow jams. Other types of CD's I manufactured were the "Old School Classics," and "Hip Hop Classics." Given my music background, I excelled at making CDs that people wanted to hear, which included a variety of genres. Every week, I would go to local barber shops and hair salons to sell my CDs. Before I knew it, I had become the neighborhood "CD man." Although I was generating a decent income from making and selling CDs, I hated every minute of it. At times, I felt embarrassed and even somewhat guilty about selling CDs as a means of income rather than working a regular nine to five job. Nevertheless, my children were my main priority and I knew that I had to do whatever it took to provide for my family. Even though I was selling CDs, I was working hard and not completely bootlegging mainstream music. Well, at least that was the case until Napster arrived on the scene.

Napster was one of the first online music sharing services. The creation of Napster sent me into a tailspin. The digital music revolution began with Napster and it instantly cut into my profits. Napster made it easy for people to find music for themselves at the click of a mouse. Even if the music was obscure or out of print, it could be found through services like Napster. This forced me, yet again, to begin doing something that I vowed never to do. Not long after, I started burning copies of mainstream full-length music CDs. Basically, I was creating bootleg copies of popular music and selling it on the streets. At the time, I thought there were no governing laws against burning CDs, as long as "For Promotional Use Only" was clearly labeled on the front cover. Not long after I began this activity, police task force raided one of the stores through which I distributed my CDs. The owner was arrested and given a heavy fine. This was an obvious sign that my days of selling bootleg CDs were coming to an end.

Selling CDs is not exactly the proudest time of my life, but it helped my family survive. Slowly, I managed to move us from our one-bedroom apartment to a two bedroom. My kids were now sleeping in bunkbeds. They slept two to a bunk rather than on blankets in the living room. After that, we graduated to a three-bedroom house. Finally, we had enough space for my family of five. The only problem was, the place was a complete dump. We dealt with mice and roach infestations. Moreover, parts of the house always seemed to be falling apart. To add even more insult to injury, we had a slumlord. She vowed to make the necessary repairs to the home, but that never happened. Despite her lack of maintaining the property, she promptly demanded the rent money when it was due. She had no reservation about showing up on my doorstep, unannounced the minute rent was due. She made constant threats to evict us even if I was just a day late on the rent.

I was at home one Sunday Afternoon watching football. I am a huge fantasy football fan and I had three televisions set up in my living room so we could watch multiple games at one time. Darrell and another good friend, Mike Clipp were there watching the games with me. Earlier that week, I put out poisonous mice bait to help control the mice infestation. While we were watching the football games, mice came running into the living from every corner all of a sudden. I could not believe what we were seeing. It was obvious that they had eaten some of the mouse pellets because they were wobbling around. Unquestionably, I knew it was time to find another house.

During my slumlord days, I started dating a young lady with whom I coached basketball. She had three kids of her own and our relationship moved relatively fast. It was not long after we started dating that we decided to live together. Initially, she was going to move into the mice and roach infested house with me. However, we decided that moving into a cleaner, safer home would be in our best interest. We also needed more space. We eventually found a home and moved in. It had four bedrooms and was quite spacious. To my surprise, my children did not like her at all. Soon after we moved in together, I found out that she suffered from bipolar disorder. This explained why she would sometimes be the kindest person, but the next moment could be cold and callous. Needless to say, that relationship didn't last. After our break-up, I was left with the responsibility of paying for rent and utilities on my own. We had moved into the four-bedroom house after agreeing upon shared responsibility for the rent and bills, but then I became totally accountable for everything. Once again, I needed to figure out how I was going to manage all the bills without any assistance. This time, I had an understanding landlord. His name was Sigmund and without a doubt, he was the best landlord I ever had. Sigmund had a heart of gold and he understood my struggles. He knew that I was a single dad raising four kids and he always looked out for me. There was a time that I was three months behind on my rent. Sigmund allowed me to pay what I could until I got caught up. He was a lifesaver and genuinely good person. I have much gratitude for his generosity at a time when it was greatly needed.

As a father, I tried to learn from what I perceived as my dad's mistakes with my upbringing. I avoided bringing a woman into my life just to take care of my kids. Since my dad worked long hours, he needed help rearing me. Because of that experience, I wanted to make sure that I raised my kids myself. I wanted to be present when they needed me. I did not want to put the onus on someone else to raise my children. Although I cohabitated with a few of the females I dated, they were never responsible for rearing my children. I was always visible and made most of the decisions in the home. The next young lady I dated lived in the home with me, but she was somewhat high maintenance. I continued to pay all of the bills, tried my best to cater to her wants, and needs. Physically, she lived in the home with us, but she always seemed mentally checked out. I tried to make sure that she had the finer things that she desired. In essence, I was always working to impress her. This made no sense at all since I was not financially sound. Like someone that has found their first love, I was smitten and not thinking straight. While we were together, I came to the decision that I wanted to stop selling mix CDs. This was a choice that I knew would severely diminish my income. I was trying to lead by example and teach my kids about integrity. I realized that I could not tell them to do the right thing while I was doing the exact opposite. Therefore, I set myself a stop date, that way I'd have enough time to get everything in order before making the change.

Once I made this decision, I went to my lady friend and told her about my plan. I thought since I'd helped her through school, provided her with a place to live and supported her while she worked towards her nursing degree, that she could provide similar support in my time of need. By this time, she had graduated from a nursing program and was earning a decent wage. Unfortunately, she was not receptive to my request to help out with the bills until I established another means of income. Instead, she informed me that she did not consider herself as actually living in our home. Basically, she laughed in my face. In that moment, I realized something: people can be in the same car as you, but that does not mean they're riding for you. From there, our relationship slowly deteriorated. Eventually we went our separate ways and I vowed to myself that, moving forward, I would work toward getting my own affairs in order before bringing anyone else into my life. My first priority remained taking care of my kids and to maintain food and shelter. When I look back on those days, I just shake my head. There was nothing easy about raising four kids alone. I had no "real job" and unlike some, I did not have my mother around to help out when needed. My stepmother and I did not have a relationship and my dad was much too busy to babysit. Overall, it was just very hard. To this day, I tell my kids, I don't know how we made it through, but by the grace of God, we did.

CHAPTER

(The Birth of Coach Freddy Fri)

"I stopped hooping 10th grade never knew back then"
"I'd be a coach not worried if we lose or win"
"Make winning be reflected by the lesson you learn"
"That ensures in due time many blessings you earn"
Lyrics taken from verse 3 of
Playya 1000 and The Deeksta's song "Dreams"
(Full song available on all streaming platforms)

During my "young and dumb" years, my cousin Willie would say, "Your common sense meter was pretty low"! It was my birthday and I had just turned twenty-one years old. Darrell and I went to a local club to celebrate. At the club, I met a young lady and we immediately hit it off. She was a few years older than me, but a really cool person. She is the same young lady I mentioned earlier who had five kids of her own. I could barely take care of the one child I had at the time, let alone adding five more. People in my circle told me to leave her alone, but I did not listen. I was still living young and reckless and had not yet experienced my epiphany. Nevertheless, we wasted no time becoming an official couple. Her kids were young when we met and they instantly gravitated towards me. I still have a close bond with her children today. She had three daughters and two sons. Her oldest son was a phenomenal athlete. He excelled in both football and basketball. When he was in middle school, I took him to sign up for basketball. As it turns out, the school was looking for a volunteer assistant coach. They wanted someone to help the head coach manage the team and attend the games.

When I played basketball in school, I had a natural knack for coaching my teammates while on the floor. I always had this underlying ability to coach. Thus, the volunteer assistant coach position peaked my interest. I promptly inquired about the position and was ultimately chosen as the assistant coach. The following year, I was given the opportunity to serve as head coach for the sixth grade "B" team. The school for which I was coaching historically had not achieved much success with their basketball program. However, I was determined to change that. I was meticulous, paying attention to every detail; the little things that most people overlook. I was focused and completely locked in on creating one of the best teams the school had ever had. I always prepared my team to function at their highest capacity. I assessed the strengths and weaknesses of each player and used that information to design an efficient team. I led that sixth grade "B" team to an undefeated record for the school year. Subsequently, we played in the championship game, but lost to one of the top programs in the city. Even though we lost, we were actually winners. It was an amazing season for the players because they had never experienced that level of success. I occasionally see some of those kids today and they always speak of the fond memories of that winning season.

After I had so much success as a "B" coach, the school gave me the opportunity to serve as the "A" coach the following year. This time, I had more experienced players. Only eight teams were selected to move on to the playoffs that year, and we were among those eight. In the quarterfinals, we upset the undefeated champs of the previous year. I always emphasized that doing the little things is what puts a team in the position to win games. That is exactly what happened in that game. We did the little things and emerged victorious. After winning that particular game, I gained a lot of respect in coaching circles and amongst my peers. Years later, I would see the coach of the team we defeated in the quarterfinals. He said to me, "Coach I still remember you beating me and ruining my chance of having back to back undefeated seasons." He went on to say "I remember thinking who is this young dude coaching this team"? He also said, "I had really good players and for your team to beat us, you had to coach your butt off"! I just laughed and replied "thanks coach."

At the end of the season, the boys asked me if I would continue to coach them to help them compete at the level of AAU/Club ball. Back then, I knew very little about AAU sports or tournament dynamics. However, when they asked, I got that itch again so I agreed. I became even more of a mentor to those boys than I already had been. I was more than just a coach; I was a role model. There were many inner city kids on my team and I would provide rides to practice and games. Similar to the goals for my own kids, my goal for the players was to keep them surrounded by positive influences and away from harm and negativity. During rides to practices or games, the boys wanted to listen to hardcore rap. I would always halt that behavior. I would tell them that I was trying to show them a different side of life. My goal was to keep everything positive and productive.

I eventually created an AAU team comprised of some of my school players and a few players from other schools. Next, we needed a name for our team. In my distribution company name, I used the word "federal," which represented the top level of government. At that time in the hip-hop world, the buzzword was *ballin'*. Everybody wanted to be a "big baller." Hence, I came up with the name Federal Ballerz. Instead of spelling it B-A-L-L-E-R-S, I chose to add a "Z" at the end just to give it a little more pizzazz. As far as I knew, we were the only team called the Ballerz back then. Fast forward to today and there are hundreds of teams with the name. However, we were the originals, at least locally. After our team started playing, I stumbled across a player whose dad was well off. The father invested in our team and rented a greyhound bus for us travel to a tournament in Kansas. My team went to that tournament and actually won the championship. They were bouncing off the walls because we managed to make a comeback in the last three minutes of the game from an eleven-point deficit to win the championship. I was as equally elated. I had made many huge accomplishments in a short period of time as a basketball coach.

Around the same time, my oldest daughter had just reached the third grade. I was still dating the young lady with the five kids on and off. She also had a daughter in third grade. I had already been working with both girls teaching them how to play basketball. However, it did not come easy to them. Making matters worse, I did not entirely understand just how much time, effort, and patience it takes to learn the intricacies of the game of basketball. I was very hard on them as we practiced in the front yard. I couldn't understand why they had difficulty making a perfect lay-up or using the correct technique in dribbling the basketball. In due time, I learned that nothing in the game of basketball comes easy. Becoming a high-level player takes consistent practice over a course of time. Now that I am wiser and much more knowledgeable about the game of basketball, I chuckle when parents become frustrated that their kid is not an overnight sensation. Most just do not understand that it takes long, hard, consistent work to become an elite basketball player.

As for my oldest daughter, I noticed that she could run fast. In addition, my lady friend's daughter was very tall. They were both learning how to play basketball so I decided to form a recreation team using girls in the community. At the time, most men did not want to coach girls because they would need to employ a different coaching approach. They would have to be a bit more toned down and softer in their speech and mannerisms. Furthermore, girls need more time with the fundamentals of the game. Generally, girls learn the game of basketball differently from boys. Personally, I love teaching the fundamentals of the game. I see it as a challenge to teach a novice player the basics of the game and then mold them into an excellent player. That is the uniqueness to girls' basketball. I began teaching and molding my "rec" team. Eventually, we began competing in AAU tournaments. Needless to say, we were getting our butts kicked at first. Even so, the girls did not quit. They kept working hard, getting better and focusing on the little things that I spoke about before.

I saw vast improvements in my team while coaching the young ladies, but I struggled with asking parents for payment for my services. Early on, I had not developed the proper coaching structure that included fees for tournaments, gym time and coaching. Typically, team dues covered hotel rooms for the coach, travel expenses and entry fees for tournaments. Unfortunately, I never constructed any type of payment guidelines for my team. I was trying to manage it all out of pocket. I quickly learned that if you do not ask, people do not know and therefore, do not give. My mistake was putting on a front as if I was doing okay financially. The reality of the situation is financially, I was in a crisis. Nonetheless, our team was performing well in the AAU tournaments. We did so well that an opportunity was extended to represent Oklahoma at AAU nationals in Kingsport, Tennessee. The girls were in sixth grade. I was still driving my beat down mini-van, and I was afraid it might not make it to Tennessee. Luckily, after fifteen hours of driving, we eventually made it to AAU nationals. However, about midway, the sliding door broke on my mini-van. I had to rig it shut so that it would not fly open during the remainder of the trip. I was still selling mixed CDs at the time so I had to bring my CD burner on the trip and make sure there was a postal service nearby. That way, I could continue shipping out CDs as a means of generating income. I absolutely could not afford to lose any potential earnings. I often think back about how crazy those times were.

My goal for the AAU National tournament was to at least finish as one of the top sixteen teams. We achieved the goal, but after several days of being in Kingsport, I was running out of money. I was so broke that I could not afford for us to win another game! Winning again would mean staying another night in the hotel and I just did not have the money for it. It also meant paying for meals and other incidentals. We were gearing up for our next game, which was against another very good team. We actually managed to carve out a decent lead against that team. Shortly before halftime, I looked over at my sidelines and noticed that we still had two girls on the bench who had not yet stepped on the floor. They looked so sad and my heart went out to them. Since we had a bit of a lead, I decided to put them both in the game. Immediately, my parents began to protest. One shouted, "It is too soon for lower skilled players to enter the game"! Yet, I put them in the game. Within two minutes, we lost the lead and never regained our momentum. Everyone was bummed out that we lost, but that loss saved me from being forced to borrow money from someone to pay for another night's hotel stay.

The next time we went to nationals, I was determined to figure out an alternate means of paying for our trip. That is when fundraising became a priority. I arranged a number of fundraising techniques with the team, which put us in a much better place financially. A few years later, we earned our way back to AAU nationals, but this time it was held in Minnesota. Since we were from a small city in Oklahoma, no one viewed us as a serious competitor. We were undoubtedly the underdogs. Early on, we played a team from Long Beach, California who placed in the top four in the country the previous year. In the beginning, they were destroying us. They were leading twenty-six points to our mere four points. To put it lightly, I was livid. I called a time out and ripped into the girls. I told them not to be scared. I reminded them that we worked hard and were fully prepared for this moment. The other team had a girl who would later go on to play in the Women's National Basketball Association (WNBA). She was a very skilled player and the main source of our troubles in that game. As I studied how to contain her, I noticed that she had trouble dribbling the basketball with her left hand. I decided to use that insight to our advantage. I told my girls to force her left, after which she would try to do a spin move. When she tried to spin, one of my girls would be ready to take the ball from her. My girls executed that strategy to perfection and it was a turning point of that game.

Our game plan took the future WNBA player so far out of her element that her confidence was shattered. With her out of commission, the rest of the team followed suit. We eventually took the lead and won that game. We continued to win even more games afterwards. Random coaches were following me around trying to figure out how we were winning so many games. We were the outliers; just a small team from Tulsa, Oklahoma, playing against teams from big cities where they recruited all of the best players from their region to represent their state. People could not understand how a group of girls from a small city were dominating the way we were. We ultimately finished third in the nation that year. That was a very strong team from which many of the girls went on to play for notable colleges such as UCLA, Tennessee, Georgetown, Baylor and Oral Roberts University. They all went on to do phenomenal things in their lives and in their careers.

That was just the beginning of my basketball program for coaching girls. From there, I established the Federal Ballerz program, which became a non-profit organization. Since then, we have continued to support the personal growth of student athletes, provide mentorship, and opportunities for student athletes to attend college through athletic scholarships. Youth basketball has grown from predominately-competitive AAU teams into a system that features club teams that recruit the best players for shoe circuits like Nike, Adidas, and Under Armor, to play in front of hundreds of college coaches. Youth basketball and youth sports in general is very big business. Over the years playing in different events, I began analyzing how the businesses were operated. I observed entry fee amounts, and researched the number of teams in each age group, number of spectators, gate fees, and concession items and sales. Mentally, I completed the math and realized that these events were generating a sizeable income. I became intrigued and thought to myself, *I can do that*! Prior to that, I never thought about the business side of amateur basketball, but this would be the industry that would change my life for the better.

Throughout my years as a coach, I've always explained to my players that the game of basketball is a tool that should be used to build lasting relationships. I always stress that basketball will serve them well later in life. I emphasize that basketball is a microcosm of life. Just like life itself, it moves fast and will put you to the test if you are not prepared mentally or physically. The game of basketball teaches so many valuable life lessons. Among other lessons, it demonstrates integrity, passion, teamwork, communication and maintaining composure. That's why I love the game so much. Through basketball, I was able to build many positive relationships and a good reputation. That means the world to me. Little did I know that all of my years of coaching was equivalent to attending college or learning a trade. I truly feel that the universe blessed me because I genuinely gave from the heart and added value to so many. I had no idea of the career that was being prepared for my life. I just had a passion to coach and mentor kids. Basketball is the perfect way to teach kids many life skills. And that's why, I always make sure that my players and their parents understand that for me, it's always bigger than basketball!

CHAPTER

10

(Back to the Music)

"Ya potnas back with new rhymes"
"Riddles from the middle they get better with time"
"and that's why we back in the mix "
"I'm tryna get you to see right like an optometrist"
Lyrics taken from verse 1 of
Playya 1000 and The Deeksta's song "2 Step"
(Full song available on all streaming platforms)

While I was building the Oklahoma Federal Lady Ballerz AAU basketball brand, time seemed to fly by. All the while, I was mentoring student athletes and coaching one of the top girls' basketball teams in the country. Life was getting busier and my four little ones were now much older. Around this time, they ranged from ages eleven to fifteen. Just like most kids their age, peer pressure was becoming apparent. One of the main peer influences was listening to hip-hop music. Although I still considered myself a hip-hop artist, I had not written a rap in nearly eight years. Sad to say, the hip-hop music they liked the most was laced with negative messages and profanity. It was very different from the safe, clean songs I selected for our basketball road trip music. These mixes had kid friendly content from the likes of Will Smith, Run DMC, Rakim, New Edition and many more.

In efforts to shield my kids from negativity, I never let them listen to any of my old music. Despite the fact that most of the messages in my songs had a positive tone, many of them were filled with profanity just like mainstream hip-hop music. Over time, I learned that a strong, clear message within a song could be made without cursing and obscenities. Being solution minded, I decided to find a way to deter my kids from listening to foul music. I came up with the bright idea to create catchy, hip-hop songs with a positive vibe. I told Darrell about my plan and he was completely on board with it. We were eager to get back into the studio and start making music again. Prior to Darrell and I making that decision, he had given one of our old CDs to a local radio DJ. That particular CD featured our classic song *"Sunday Afternoon"* and to our surprise, the DJ played it on the radio. Afterwards, the radio station was flooded with calls from listeners and supporters of our music. They spoke about feelings of nostalgia and just having a good time vibing with that song once again. Shortly thereafter, I received a call from Dangerous Rob, another local hip-hip legend. We began our rap careers about the same time. He was part of the local, legendary rap groups Thob Mob and Partners-N-Rhyme. There was a time in the past when we were rivals. By the current time, we were older, more mature and actually had become good friends.

Rob called me and said that a friend of his from Texas had been trying to contact me in order to buy some of my old music. Rob informed me that he gave his friend my contact information and that I should be expecting a call from him soon. Not long after, I received a call from the man and his name was Trevor Naughton. He asked if I had any of our old music for sale, specifically our "Foe Da Mill Ticket" CD. That particular project was the last album we released before I gained custody of my kids. Trevor mentioned that he operated an online distribution service that catered to many clientele overseas. He said that whenever he asked his customers about their favorite artists, the Playya 1000 name would come up almost every time. I was taken completely by surprise. My distribution deals previously made through Federal Entertainment were nationwide, but I had no idea that the Playya 1000 brand was listened to on a global scale. I was astonished to find out that people all over the world enjoyed our music. Since the "Foe Da Mill Ticket" album was not heavily promoted, I had a ton of extra copies collecting dust in my garage. Trevor offered to buy the CDs at twenty bucks each. That amount was well above the usual wholesale value, which landed around six or seven dollars. I quickly jumped at the opportunity for making some extra income. Trevor initially requested twenty CDs, which netted me four hundred dollars. I could not believe how this blessing dropped into my lap from nowhere. I desperately needed that break and the fact that it was legal made it all the better. A week later, Trevor called me back and requested more CDs. Again, I agreed to send twenty additional CDs without question. Another week went by and he called again with another order. This time, the conversation was slightly different. He asked why I never questioned what he was doing with the CDs. I told him that I appreciated the blessing and trusted that he was not doing anything illegal. I really could not think of a reason to be concerned. After all, the CDs had just been sitting unused in my garage.

What Trevor said to me that day will never be forgotten. He said that since I seemed like such a good person, he wanted to share what he had been doing with the CDs. He then told me to go online to EBay and type in Playya 1000. What I saw that day still blows my mind. I saw people from all over the world bidding upwards of five hundred dollars for a single Playya 1000 CD. My jaw dropped. While I had been satisfied with the four hundred dollar profit from selling twenty CDs at a time, Trevor effectively made about ten thousand dollars collectively from the sale of my CDs. He would sell them in an online auction on EBay where bidding often topped out at five-hundred dollars for a *single* CD. Then, he would sell the remaining CDs as "second chance offers" to the other bidders. Simply because he believed that I was a good person, he blessed me with the opportunity and the knowledge to do the same. Undeniably, this was another instance of my mom looking out for me. She steered the universe in my favor. Over the course of time, Trevor and I formed a very fruitful, positive relationship. To this day, I thank him for being there in my time of need and sharing with us the international impact of Playya 1000 and the Deeksta music. This situation was another event that profoundly sparked my interest in recording again.

Darrell and I had a renewed sense of purpose. We were ready to begin recording our new, clean-cut music. Our fire was back! Now we just needed to find a new recording studio. Unfortunately, the process proved much more complicated than we had anticipated. First of all, changes in studio technology meant that we had to search everywhere for a studio offering reel-to-reel technology, which we were accustomed to. When we found a suitable studio, we never entirely settled in because Darrell and the studio manager had many disagreements. It was not long before we were on the hunt again for another suitable studio. Eventually, we found another studio and began revising some of our old songs by removing the profanity. We were so thrilled to be recording again that the decision was made to not only clean up the old music, but to also create brand new Playya 1000 and the Deeksta music. The new studio lasted for only a short while. It was shrouded with incompetence and a poor work environment. Furthermore, it was not uncommon to see some engineers using drugs. This was not the type of environment that Darrell and I had envisioned for ourselves. It got so bad that Darrell gave an ultimatum. He refused to work in any more menial studio environments. If we could not find a satisfactory recording studio in a high quality environment, Darrell said that he would bow out of the music game once again. Fortunately, my man Dangerous Rob came through in our time of need. He referred us to Mark Bryan, the owner of a private studio called House Recordings. Although he is legally blind, Rob told us that Mark was an incredible engineer. That introduction changed our recording environment from bleak to awesome. Gone were the dingy studios in terrible neighborhoods. Mark operated a clean, family-friendly studio with high-quality equipment. It was such a good environment; my kids could also come along whenever necessary. To sweeten the deal, Mark was a musical phenom. We still have a solid working relationship with him to this day.

Just like old times, Darrell would create a beat and I would write the lyrics. While writing one day, I came up with a song called *Two Step in The Club*. I remember writing this lyric, "Trying to get you to see right like an optometrist." At the time, I had no idea that it would become the basis for our new music project, the 20-20 Vision album. My mantra became "see the game of life with 20-20 vision." There was a time when blinders covered my eyes, but now my vision is crystal clear. Things were going great for Darrell and I so we decided to take our fan favorite song, "Sunday Afternoon" and record a remix. At that time, our local radio station, KJAMZ 105 was celebrating their ten-year anniversary. Since one of the first songs they played was our original version of "Sunday Afternoon," we decided to send them our remix. As expected, KJAMZ 105 played the new version of "Sunday Afternoon" and again it became a hit. After so many years away from the game, we felt our career had been resurrected. Consequently, we conducted performances at local venues and various parties while focusing on positive messages through music. From there, I started a new project called Hip Hop Motivation. This was a project that I performed as a soloist. I would visit local inner city schools and spread positive messages to the students through my rap lyrics. Although donations were requested to cover expenses, I virtually did these performances for free. It felt amazing to give back to the community and add value to so many lives. It felt even more incredible to achieve my goal of making clean-cut rap lyrics that my kids enjoyed.

As Darrell and I continued to make new music, another flattering opportunity presented itself that we could have never predicated. I received a call from an online distributor of out-of-print music. The man's name was Shu and he lived in Yokohama,

Japan. Not only did Shu begin buying our old CDs for resale in his brick and mortar store, but also he gave us a life-changing opportunity to perform in Japan. Shu informed us that there was a huge following in Japan of Playya 1000 and the Deeksta music. He wanted us to perform in Yokohama in front of a crowd that was fully expected to be sold out. To say that we were shocked is an understatement. Darrell and I were in total disbelief. However, we happily found ourselves in Yokohama, Japan a few months later. We performed in front of a hyped, sold-out crowd who vibed to our music all night. We met so many genuine, diehard fans. We signed autographs, took pictures and watched grown men and women cry upon meeting us. It was one of the most exhilarating and unforgettable time of our lives.

Admittedly, the Yokohama experience was somewhat a test of wills. Darrell and I are very down-to-earth people and we were more than happy to hang out with our fans after the show. In return, our fans wanted to show us a really good time. We received endless offers for free drinks and other gratuities. As I have shared before, I pride myself on never have taken a drink or smoked in my life. I also understood that the crowd of people were just showing their appreciation for our music through offering free drinks. I am pleased that I stayed strong and true to my morals. Although I respected the act of gratitude, I remained alcohol-free that night. Even so, being in Japan was a phenomenal experience. This would eventually pave the way for another unbelievable opportunity.

In Downtown Tulsa, there is an amazing placed called Guthrie Green. It is a community town square that is used to celebrate the performing arts. Every year, an Old School Hip-Hop show is held at Guthrie Green in which local and mainstream artists are featured. In the summer of 2019, another Old School Hip-Hop show was scheduled to be held at Guthrie Green. Even though we were not initially slated to perform at the show, another local rap artist named Steph Simon, asked us to be part of his set. He shared that we were one of his favorite rap artists and he wanted to pay homage by allowing us to perform. The show featured artists such as Big Daddy Kane, MC Lyte, Slick Rick, and Roxane Shante. During Steph's set, in front of around six thousand fans, he brought us out. Pandemonium broke out over the crowd as we began performing the fan favorite, "*Sunday Afternoon.*" It was one of the most powerful moments in our career, especially because it was performed in our hometown. The energy in the crowd was astounding. The vibe was palpable and I cannot put into words what it felt like to have everyone sing each word of the song along with us.

All of the big breaks we received after resurrecting our rap career made it worth every minute that we had devoted to reinventing ourselves. Thinking back to elementary school when I was too shy to speak in public and had no interest in performing music outside of my own bedroom, I could not imagine that my music would touch the masses. Simply by overcoming my fear of public speaking and reaching beyond my comfort zone, I was able to share with the world my talent and my message. Thanks to the choice of overcoming fear, I have put myself in the positon of being a leader, an influencer. I realized that there is an opportunity to lead by example and show other up and coming artists how to give back to the people, the community. I believe we all have a purpose for leaving the world better than we found it. As I look back on my many years recording music and writing lyrics, it is clear that hip-hop was and still is a driving force in my life. It is an outlet to release stress and manage anxiety. Currently, music lives in me. It is a part of my existence. Making good music has morphed into an entertaining hobby for Darrell and I. We record and release music whenever it drives us and when we find the extra time. To this day, our goal with music is to spread positivity and to provide uplifting words of encouragement. From being just two, insignificant young boys from the hood, we are honored that our music has made a difference in the lives of so many people and that it continues to have a lasting impact on the world.

CHAPTER

(The Birth of Court Time Events)

"Now I tell 'em they were born to be spectacular"
"Court Time diplomat I'm the ambassador"
"It seems overnight, but it took me many moons"
"Dark days I had to overcome the doom and gloom"
Lyrics taken from verse 2 of
Playya 1000 and The Deeksta's song "First Class"
(Full song available on all streaming platforms)

At this point, my life had become a juggling act. I was trying to manage raising kids, recording music, coaching basketball and all the while still hustling to make ends meet. By now, my kids were old enough to stay home alone, so I finally started working a traditional job. From six in the morning to two o'clock in the afternoon, five days a week, I worked as a telephonic customer service technician for DirecTV. Although I still maintained an entrepreneurial mindset, my life had become bogged down with work and coaching. I was still having success as a coach and became intrigued with the idea of hosting my own youth basketball tournaments. Back then, the top local tournaments were ran by an organization called Hardwood Productions. After playing in one of their tournaments, I casually mentioned to one of my player's dad that I was seriously considering my own events. When I told him this, his eyes lit up. Apparently, he had been considering the same thing for some time. This particular parent also had a background of coaching basketball. We both noticed that a good income could potentially be made with hosting tournaments; and the market was wide open. We developed a partnership through verbal agreement. We were starting from ground zero, the basics. We had absolutely no resources or connections to secure viable gym space. However, we decided to stay the course and identify the right people to consult in this new venture. Being a new start-up, we decided to follow the model of Hardwood Productions, just on a smaller scale. Needless to say, it was an uphill climb. We still needed to arrange agreements for renting basketball courts, hire referees and clock workers; and individuals to manage the concession stand. Since we both had teenage children, we figured that we had the workforce covered. We would simply put our children to work. Yet, we still needed to promote our events in a way that attracted teams to come play in our tournaments. We also needed to decide when and where to host our first event. Hardwood Productions would always have the best gyms and dates booked for their tournaments. Since we were just starting, we were not exactly competitive in that area. We also greatly respected the Hardwood Productions tournament director. Thus, we planned our events around theirs by avoiding overlapping any of their dates.

Whenever Hardwood Productions was not having a tournament, we would have ours. Once that was established, we began developing relationships in securing gym space. Initially, it was very difficult to rent any of the premium gyms because they were already taken. That left us with less desirable gyms in a sketchy part of town. Our first gym was located in a small community center named Ben Hill. Sometimes, there would be a panhandler who would hang around the gym entrance and ask our customers for money. This was very annoying and not a good impression for our tournament. A $99 entry fee special was offered for our very first tournament. In addition to other locations, we handed out flyers at the Hardwood tournaments to attract clientele. Thankfully, Hardwood's director did not seem to mind. For our first event, eight teams registered and we were super-excited. The tournament went well and we were on our way to being credible tournament directors. After the many operational issues at Ben Hill Community Center, we moved our tournaments to another gym called Owen Park. To be honest, the place was not exactly an upgrade from Ben Hill. It was more like a lateral move. One weekend during our tournament, someone actually stole the tires off the car of one of our customers. This happened late in the evening, but in the middle of a crowded parking lot. To this day, I still cannot fathom how that happened. From there, we moved to another place called Lacy Park. This was a short-lived arrangement. A few days after one of our tournaments there, a man was murdered in their parking lot. Although we continued to build relationships, we had much difficulty attracting top teams to our tournaments because the gym locations were less than ideal.

Thankfully, our hard work and persistence paid off. Through a connection, we eventually met a man who set up a meeting with an individual who worked at one of the local high schools. The school was Central High School. Its location worked in our favor and the gym facilities were nice. Once Central High School became the primary spot for our basketball tournaments, business improved for our tournaments. We formed such a great relationship with the school's athletic director that we were offered co-head coaching jobs for the upcoming basketball season. Gladly, we accepted the offer. This arrangement not only allowed continued use of the school's facilities for our events, but it also afforded us a hefty discount in renting the gym for our weekend tournaments. As co-head coaches for Central High School girls' basketball team, we did quite well. We took a previously losing team to a playoff victory the following year.

This was something that hadn't been achieved in over twenty years at that school. This was another momentous time of my life. Unfortunately our time at Central High School was short lived. The athletic director took a position at another school and our contracts were not renewed. Once again, we faced the problem of securing appropriate venues for our tournaments. Tulsa Public Schools (TPS) in general were no longer allowing gyms to be rented for private basketball tournaments. The athletic director for TPS was in the middle of a scandal regarding usage of athletic facilities at various schools. This was a big story in Oklahoma and was all over the news. The Federal Bureau of Investigation (FBI) became involved and many people affiliated with management of TPS gym facilities were called to testify under oath about rental arrangements. After that, it became virtually impossible for anyone to rent TPS gymnasiums.

Even though our outlook was bleak on obtaining good gym facilities, we caught another break. After some time had passed, we were able to arrange an agreement with a few prime facilities just outside of Tulsa and with Oral Roberts University. From these arrangements, we were once again holding our tournaments in superior facilities. The only problem was I found myself still struggling financially. What I had hoped would turn into a major source of income was still just a side hustle. I was three months behind on my rent and could not seem to catch up on my bills. We were making some progress, but hosting events once or twice per month was not generating enough income to provide for my family. It wasn't much longer before I began considering the notion of holding tournaments on my own. Proactively, I devised a blueprint for success as an owner of a sole proprietorship.

When I was ready, I informed my business partner of the decision to branch out on my own. We agreed that he would keep the company name. In addition, I told him that he could keep all the proceeds in our business account. I was starting fresh and anew. Getting honest with myself, I performed a self-assessment, identified my strengths and weaknesses, and identified problematic areas as it related to the tournament business. Thereafter, I established solutions for each problem. Primarily, I faced the fact that doing things someone else's way had not been working for us at all. Following the model of Hardwood Productions was fine when we first started, but we never put our own touches on the business. Additionally, I came to grips with the realization that after three years of hosting basketball tournaments, my financial situation had not improved. I was still working at DirectTV, still three months behind on rent, and still struggling to make ends meet.

As a coach, I would often hear complaints from parents about games being scheduled on Sundays. People generally prefer to use Sunday as a day of rest, for church, or to spend time with their families. Although this was a common complaint, there were no basketball tournaments being hosted as one-day events in the Tulsa area. To separate myself from the others, I examined holding a basketball tournament on Saturday only. This would leave Fridays and Sundays open to families to use for their personal time. Next, I considered my tournament dates. If you recall, up until this point, our events were planned to avoid overlapping with the Hardwood tournaments. For that reason, we would host tournaments only once or twice each month. For my new business model, I figured that I could schedule tournaments every week on Saturdays and allow the individual teams to decide which Saturday they wanted to play or they could play every Saturday if they desired. My overall goal was to host at least 50 tournaments each year. Excellence in customer service was my next goal. I wanted to establish definite actions that would keep teams coming back to my tournaments. As a result, I decided I would make my tournaments very schedule request friendly. If a team could only play within a certain time frame, that is when I would schedule them to play. If they needed to be finished by a certain time, I also made that happen. I have always functioned with the mentality that "the customer is always right" and I would work earnestly in satisfying their requests. The final action that propelled my business in existence was sending out text blasts to solicit basketball teams. Rather than picking up the phone and calling each coach individually, I started sending out text notifications, which saved a great deal of time and effort. At the time, this practice was uncommon. Once I made all of those changes, my job became much easier. It was mind blowing how quickly things turned around for me.

Court Time Events was the name that I chose for my basketball tournament company. It was catchy and has now become widely known in Tulsa and surrounding areas. I was a bit surprised to have a massive number of people in my corner, rooting me on and wondering what had taken me so long to branch out on my own. My new business venture took off and every decision, every change that I made worked in my favor. Teams and coaches had come to expect my weekly tournaments and they actually started calling me, asking to register. My little side hustle quickly became a fully functioning business thanks to my ability to think outside the box and be solution-minded. I was able to leave DirectTV, leave behind all of my side hustles, and generate enough income to support my family. Since then, Court Time Events has become massively successful, all because I chose to bet on myself. More importantly, I took several calculated steps before branching out. I also made sure to have realistic, measurable goals. Effectively, I was fully prepared when the time came to transition. When I finally did take that leap of faith, I had already put myself in a position to hit on my bet. And, that's exactly what happened. Little did I know that all of those years of mentoring kids and adding value to others would eventually be rewarded by the universe in the form of my youth basketball business: Court Time Events.

CHAPTER

12

(Bachelor's Degree at Age 43)

"43 college handed me my bachelors"
"Sorry ladies, but no longer I'm a bachelor"
"Now I tell them they were born to be spectacular"
"Court Time diplomat I'm the ambassador"
Lyrics taken from verse 2 of
Playya 1000 and The Deeksta's song "First Class"
(Full song available on all streaming platforms)

The blessing of my newfound success with Court Time Events (CTE) propelled me into the unfamiliar territory of having a little extra money. As someone who struggled financially, I never take anything for granted. I am always looking for opportunities to create alternate streams of income. With no trade or college degree, I had a heart-to-heart session with myself and considered other options of sustainability. Although CTE was doing well, there was no guarantee that it would consistently be profitable. I had just embarked on my own and did not know what the future held for CTE. For several years, I contemplated returning to school and finishing my degree. I estimated that CTE would most likely be profitable for at least three additional years. I figured that timeframe would allow for returning to school. My goal was to obtain a bachelor's degree in education and become a teacher. I figured that if CTE ever dissolved, I would be in the position to begin a teaching career. I would no longer be relegated to low-paying jobs in which I had no interest.

I had already completed a year of college so there was a good chance of receiving credit for some of those classes. As I continued to navigate through the steps of going back to college, there was one huge problem: My mountain of student loan debt was coming back to haunt me. If you recall, in my young and reckless days, I enrolled in College of America and accepted loan money then quickly dropped out of school. That mistake was coming back to bite me. When I applied for financial aid and attempted to enroll in classes, I was informed that I owed a substantial amount in student loans. Since I failed to pay my loans, they had gone into default. That meant before I could even think about enrolling in school, I needed to take the proper steps in emerging from default status. Luckily for me, the loan offices were more than willing to work with me. They told me that I could bring my loans out of default if I agreed to enroll in a payment plan. In order to do this, I was required to make a fixed payment each month without being late or missing a payment. They even allowed me to choose the amount that I could afford. I set up the payment plan and by the end of that year; I emerged out of default and was finally allowed to enroll in classes.

Before enrolling, I had to determine which classes would be credited. Thereafter, a degree plan was drafted and I was officially a college student again! I decided to attend Tulsa Community College (TCC) because they offered an associate's degree. Pursuing an associate's degree was strategic because it allowed me to gain a quick, small win as I worked towards the bachelor's degree. After a year of classes, I was the proud recipient of an associate's degree and I couldn't have been happier. That was a very proud moment. It felt good to have a degree to frame and put on my wall. It proved that my hard work and tenacity was paying off.

Having completed my associate's degree, I then looked to pursue a bachelor's degree. My first order of business was to decide which school to attend. A friend had told me that if I wanted to teach, that Northeastern State University (NSU) had the best teaching program in the state of Oklahoma. With that knowledge, I decided to enroll. I was even able to obtain a bit of grant money, which was an added bonus. I was focused and disciplined in the bachelor's program. I was attending ground courses as well as online courses. This was my first encounter with online courses, which required good organization in order to be successful. Because of that, the online courses were a bit of a struggle at first. However, I quickly got into the swing of things. Once I started studying in an intentional manner, I discovered that college was not as difficult as I had once believed. As long as I was willing to put in the time and effort, I could be successful. I also learned that having a firm understanding of the expectations of my teachers was critical to my success. In addition, from the course syllabus, I was able to determine which professors had more of a firm behavior and which professors were more lax. This gave me insight on how I might need to approach my assignments. It was a delicate balancing act, but once I mastered it, school became much more manageable. I would recommend this method to anyone attending or considering going back to college as an adult.

Completing the required clinicals and internships was the toughest thing that I encountered in my program. I was assigned to a local elementary school in Tulsa and served as the teacher's aide. My main purpose was to observe and learn the teacher's education style. From that, I could develop my own. The process itself was not too difficult. I had just grown used to being on my own time during the week. When anything disrupted my schedule, it felt like a major inconvenience. Still, I maneuvered through my classes, completed the assigned weekly observations and worked my way up to the final semester. Education students were required to serve a full internship in the final semester. This meant that for an entire semester, I would essentially be the teacher in a classroom. I was dreading the thought of doing a full internship. Because I moved around frequently during the week, I did not think I could be in one place for a full eight hours. To worsen matters, I was assigned to shadow a teacher that I felt was a bit unbalanced. Friends and family kept encouraging me to stay the course. I was told that I could prevail, no matter the situation. At first, I did not believe them. It all felt unbearable. However, every day, I followed the same schedule as my preceptor, who was the regular teacher of the class. I arrived at the school when she did, stayed late when she had to, and eventually taught some classes on my own.

Somehow, I made it through the first day, then the second, then the third. After a week, I was becoming acclimated to school, my preceptor and the environment. I created my own routine and adjusted as needed. I remembered that in life when things are uncomfortable, growth occurs. I finally settled in and knew that I would make it as my friends and family had told me. It did not take long for me to realize, however, that the teacher I was studying under was suffering from a severe case of burnout. She was a veteran teacher of more than twenty years, but it was obvious that she could not relate to the students and lacked the motivation and patience to even try. She was constantly micro managing everything and instead of putting out fires, she poured gasoline directly on them. She would be in the hallways provoking students, searching for problems and creating even more problems. The students did not like her at all and I often found myself serving as the mediator between them. I conducted frequent talks with various students in keeping them from disrespecting her.

I taught seventh and eighth grade students, but they behaved more as if they were immature adults. For the most part, these kids were from low income households. They were usually rowdy, but I was able to serve as a calming force in the classroom. I could always settle them down when the regular teacher couldn't. The students quickly grew to respect me because they knew it was bigger than just their education, I also cared about them personally. One day, I did not shadow my preceptor due to a required class at my college, NSU. I later heard that the students in my class were a little more rowdy that usual. I am told that they were banging their hands and pencils on their desks and chanting, "We want Mr. Fri"! They did this for a while until my preceptor finally managed to calm them down. The students liked me so much that my preceptor decided to use it to her advantage. When it was time for her to be evaluated by the students, she told them that since I was the one teaching the class, they should fill out the forms as if they were rating me. This would essentially boost her ratings, which undoubtedly would have been damaging to her performance as a teacher. Although her request worked in her favor, it was completely inappropriate and unethical.

Although I enjoyed teaching, so many crazy things happened in that class. There was one kid in particular who would never do his classwork. Because of this, I was trying to make a connection with him to correct that behavior. I was made aware that he had already been in some trouble outside of school. I tried everything I could, telling him that since he was already at school, he might as well do the work and pass his classes. I offered to help him along the way to get him on the right track. At one point, I felt like I was very close to a breakthrough with him. However, while in class one day, he abruptly got up from his seat and moved to the back of the classroom to sit with a group of girls. I wasn't sure what he was doing back there, but I knew it wasn't good. When the class began leaving for lunch, he stayed behind. I walked to the back of the room to find out what was going on. As I got closer, I noticed a powdery residue on his desk. The principal investigated the matter and it turned out that this kid had been snorting Xanax during class. He was arrested that day at school in front of all the other students. I felt so bad for him, but hoped that he would get the necessary help that he needed. Toward the end of the semester, my NSU college professor did my final evaluation. It was a huge ordeal in which my NSU professor was scheduled to sit in my classroom and watch as I taught the class. He evaluated how I handled myself as a teacher, my style of teaching, and how I managed the class. I was very nervous because the classroom could be very disorderly. When it was all over, I can honestly say that I have never been more proud of those students. That day, they showed me just how much they respected me by being on their best behavior. I had no issues out of any of the students that day. It almost brought tears to my eyes to know they behaved well in support of me. Before I left the school for good, I made sure to let each of the students know how much that meant to me.

With the semester over and graduation looming, I felt on top of the world. I could be at ease knowing that if CTE did not thrive, I would always have the option of teaching, which would allow me to support my family. Even though CTE is still going strong, it is comforting to know that I have a contingency plan in place. When I walked across that stage to receive my bachelor's degree, I was beyond ecstatic. This is another one my unforgettable moments of life. Here I was, obtaining my bachelor's degree at age forty-three, which was twenty-five years after starting the process. I could not have been prouder of myself. I felt my mother looking down on me with the same pride I felt. It also meant the world to me that my dad watched me cross that finish line. With my bachelor's degree in hand and a successful business, I was officially on a winning streak.

CHAPTER

13

(When I Stopped Looking, Guess What I Found)

"I feel like a kid again and I'm crushing hard"

"Stress free I take it slow in the past I know that she's been scarred"

"She got my heart bar none, superstar my number one"

"Light of my life play silly games we always having fun"

Lyrics taken from verse 1 of
Playya 1000 and The Deeksta's song "Sunny Skies"
(Full song available on all streaming platforms)

As my transformation continued, I was finally at a place of peace in my life. I had recently formed a new Ballerz fifth grade girls' team and business was going good. Strangely, many of the mothers of the players on this particular team were single. I sensed that some of the mothers were interested in me, but stuck to my plan of not dating anyone in the near future. I had been through a number of unsuccessful relationships and decided that I wanted to focus on myself for a while. That is, until I met one single parent who was different from the rest. She never seemed to pay any attention to me. She would either drop her daughter off for practice or sit and watch from the bleachers. Unlike the other single mothers, she never showed any signs of flirtation. She was very attractive, quiet and respectful. Even so, I remained true to my pledge of no dating. I never viewed her in a way other than as a parent supporting her daughter in learning the game of basketball.

I was still the same old me when it came to asking people for money for my services. I had started this new basketball team and I knew that I needed to arrange a way of collecting the dues from each parent. I ultimately came up with the idea of giving parents and players the option of working my basketball tournaments as an alternative to paying monthly fees. Depending on how many hours they worked each week, they could reduce the amount of money owed each month. Most of the parents took me up on this offer, including the attractive parent who paid me no mind. There was a miscommunication one day when she was scheduled to work one of my events. She sent me a text message to find out which job position she was supposed to work. At my events, there were essentially three job options, which included working the gate taking entrance fees, working the concession, or working the clock during the games. When I received her text message asking where she was scheduled to work, I simply replied, "Front door." She never responded, but since she was at her station on time, I assumed she had received my message. I thought nothing else of it.

The next day, I received a text message from her asking if I had sent her a message the night before. Since I had not sent her any messages, I responded "no." I explained that I had only texted her the prior afternoon. She pressed on, asking if I was sure. At this point, I called her to figure out what was going on. Apparently, she received a message from me at two o'clock in the morning, one that simply read, "Front door." I told her that I had sent that text almost twelve hours before; letting her know which station, that she would be working that day. She told me that she never received my reply that afternoon. She went on to say that, she worked the door because she was told by person that she had relieved. She told me the truth was that she had assumed I had sent her the message accidentally. She thought I meant to send it to someone else for a "booty call." We both broke out into laughter. It was hilarious.

Our conversations with one another sort of grew from there. It opened up the lines of communication and we began to learn more about each other. She was incredibly cool and although our relationship was completely platonic at that time, we began forming a bond. Her daughter was tall, but her basketball game needed a lot of work. I always joke with the daughter and say "girl when I met you, you couldn't walk and chew bubble gum at the same time." Meaning, she was not very coordinated. However, she worked extremely hard and eventually developed into a great player. As her mom and I talked more, it became clear that we were both at a similar place in our lives and that our mindsets were alike. She had recently gotten out of a relationship and just like me wasn't looking to become involved with anyone.

We continued our phone conversations and periodically met for lunch. We were slowly learning even more about each other while enjoying each other's company. Although we liked hanging out with one another, neither one of us had any intentions on entering a serious relationship so we both had our guards up. She shared that she had been married years before and experienced a divorce. I had never been married and cannot say that I had ever given marriage much thought. She was doing very well for herself as a single mother. She had a degree in nursing in addition to a couple of other advanced degrees. She had her own home and was very responsible and dependable. Before either of us knew it, we were an item. As we continued to grow in our relationship, she was always accommodating when I would stay over at her home. Although I liked the room dark, I could not sleep without the sound of SportsCenter playing on TV at night. She would always cover the TV with a towel or sheet to darken the room. That way, the TV could be kept on and the background noise of

SportsCenter would help me fall asleep. She did not like sports at all and preferred quietness when she slept. However, she always made an exception for me even when she didn't have to.

We both had easy-going personalities with virtually no stress. We quickly built a relationship of trust and never questioned one another. We were both comfortable in our own skin and respected each other's differences. We never felt the need to check each other's phone, we were never jealous, and we just got along really well. Even though we are similar in many ways, we are two very different people. Even so, she was always my biggest supporter in everything I did. The times she did not agree with me, she would always let me know in a respectful manner. I also supported her decisions as a parent. She had only one kid and I made sure that even if I disagreed with any decisions that she made, I would not question that decision. We dated several years before marrying. During the bulk of that time, we continued to live in separate households. However, I would spend most of my time at her home because my kids were transitioning from high school to college.

As time passed and our relationship grew, she made it increasingly clear that she did not want to be shacking up for the rest her life. I had never been married and was comfortable with the way things were. Eventually, we moved in together and I began to notice changes within. All of a sudden, without any forcing or prodding from her, I found that I was not sleeping with SportsCenter on anymore. Somehow, we swapped the noise from the television with the Joel Osteen channel on XM radio. I also found myself brushing my teeth twice a day and flossing regularly. All of a sudden, I realized that she was making me a better man and I was not going anywhere. That is when I decided to pop the big question.

It was Christmas Eve and we were opening presents. I gave my future wife a large sized present to open. It was a large box with a smaller box inside and an even smaller box inside of that one and so on. She had to open several boxes before getting to the final, tiny box, which was the one with the ring. I asked my youngest daughter to record the entire gift unwrapping on my phone so I could catch my future wife's reaction on camera. The box with the ring came with a note that read, "You're the love of my life. Will you marry me"? At first, she was not sure if it was real; she kept saying, "Are you serious"? She finally said yes when she knew that I was dead serious. Before her, I never thought I would get married. She was one of a kind. She changed my life and perspective on so many things for the better. People told us that once we got married that things would change, but I am happy so say they have not. To this day, we remain the same no-stress, respectful, loving couple that we have been for years. We give each other space when needed and we never let a disagreement divide us. We have been a couple for ten strong years and happily married for the last three of those ten years. I couldn't imagine my life without her. She is another one the greatest blessings in my life!

I speak to people who have just gotten out of a relationship all the time. Many of them are eager to immediately develop a new relationship with someone else. I tell them to stop looking for love. Work on yourself first and you will eventually find that person that is meant for you, the person of your dreams. That is exactly what happened to me. I can honestly say without hesitation that my wife, Lisa Frierson is the love of my life and my true soulmate. I had no idea what our relationship would become when I first met her. It was not until I stopped looking for someone that our individual worlds were united.

CHAPTER

(The Birth of Freddy Fri Motivation)

"I'm tryna get it cracking like a knuckle"
"Life so sweet it's like a honey suckle"
"Kick it with ya boys like a sensei"
"Climb the hump and make every day a WinsDay"

Lyrics taken from verse 2 of
Playya 1000 and The Deeksta's song "6-4"
(Full song available on all streaming platforms)

Ever since I had my epiphany, I've been working diligently to be the best version of myself. I bought books on how to be better organized, how to better manage time and how to be a better parent. If you came into the Frierson household back then, you'd see tons of organizational tools on the walls—chore lists, cleaning instructions and weekly schedules. Many of the things I learned from the books, I would implement then and pass on to my children. The first motivational speaker that I ever heard of was Tony Robbins. I quickly became a huge fan of his. I would purchase his audiobooks and work hard in applying his teachings to my life. Soon after, I discovered another one of my favorites: Mr. Zig Ziglar. I loved listening to his teachings because his information was practical. I loved that he was down to earth and I would always get a big laugh out of his southern accent.

The first African American speaker I started listening to was Les Brown. I actually found out about him at a music conference in New Orleans. Darrell and I had been sponsored to attend the festival for Playya 1000 and the Deeksta music. Our accommodations were made in a high-end hotel in New Orleans. One night, we decided to go workout in the gym at the hotel. When we got to the gym, we ran into none other than R&B legend, Gladys Knight. We had a phenomenal conversation with her. She told us that she was in town because her husband at that time, Les Brown was scheduled to speak at a workshop that weekend. Although she invited us to attend the workshop, our obligations to the festival prevented us from doing so. Even though I had begun following his teaching, I was not aware of how well-known Les Brown was as a motivational personality.

After that encounter, I engulfed myself in motivational materials. I was always looking to improve as an adult, a man and as a father. It was a struggle, but I was improving piece by piece, inch by inch, and minute by minute. As I got back into music, I was doing more motivational hip-hop rather than hard-core hip-hop. I created the 20/20 Movement Tour with local inner city schools. That was my first real opportunity to use hip-hop as a means of helping young students to become responsible adults. I gave them various tricks, tools and tips to help navigate the difficult situations of life. Even today, I will occasionally see some of the kids who attended my performances and they often tell how much my speech helped them. Even though I'd never thought about it in this manner, I realized that I'd been giving motivational speeches for a long time—through coaching. I had been delivering inspiring words during my pregame, halftime, postgame speeches; during practices and as motivation during time outs in the games. Even when I had to be stern or tough with my players, I prided myself on being able to communicate effectively while offering motivation and inspiration without the use of profanity.

In the midst of all of this, I remember receiving a text from a friend. It contained a link to a YouTube video. In the video, there was a guy named Eric Thomas who I'd never heard of before. He was on a football field, ranting and raving at someone. He was telling that person to stop being lazy and go be great. The entire message was really intense, but at the same time, inspiring. Thereafter, I found myself on Eric Thomas's YouTube channel binging on his other videos. It occurred to me that he was the first person I'd ever seen who was putting out motivational videos without trying to sell something. There were no affiliate links and no promotional messages. Instead, he actually gave back rather than asking to receive. He put out free motivational videos every Monday as part of his "Thank God It's Monday" (TGIM) series. This really motivated me, but it wasn't until I got deeper into writing music that the inspiration really stuck.

Around this time, Darrell and I had initiated a new project that included a song called "64". As I was writing lyrics, I came up with the line *"Kick it with your boys like a sensei,"* but I was having difficulty with writing a rhyme for the next line. Then it hit me: the word Wednesday would go in the next line. After that, I thought why not spell it W-I-N-S-D-A-Y. That way, it would represent winning every day of life. Ultimately, the line became, *"Kick it with your boys like a sensei, climb the hump and make every day a WINSday."* Immediately, I knew that was my new brand. Using my life as an example, I wanted to help people overcome their obstacles and win at life. From there, I took a cue from Eric Thomas and decided that the best strategy would be to release a video every Wednesday and call the series "Make Every Day a Winsday." I hired the same videographer that worked on my music videos Stephen Jones. I also contacted Mark Bryan at the studio to help produce the music. And just like that, I had a team of people to help me with my new brand. My goal in making these videos was never about money. I simply wanted to add as much value into people's lives as I could.

It goes without saying that my first video was nothing short of terrible. If you're curious, you can still find it on my YouTube channel. Although it was not the best video, I took a leap of faith and started the process of sharing my knowledge and story with the world. Bound by fear, some people mistakenly wait for the perfect time or opportunity to begin their idea. Please know that there is no such thing as the perfect time. If there were such a thing, that perfect time would be now. You just have to start taking steps towards your dream. The steps don't need to be monumental. They can be small, baby steps. The secret to achieving your dream is to remain diligent and consistent. In due time, the universe will work in your favor and things will spontaneously happen to help you along in your journey. I am a living testimony to this because that is exactly what happened for me! At the time, I wasn't even sure what name or moniker I wanted to go by for the WINSday videos. I was contemplating a new name when a thought struck. I remembered that during my teaching internship, the students called me Mr. Fri. The reason they did this is because most students had difficulty pronouncing my last name correctly. Rather than saying my entire name, Frierson, they shortened it to "Fri." Saying Mr. Fri was much quicker and easier for everyone. Soon after, my wife began greeting me that way as well. She was teasing me in a way, but at the same time, it was somewhat catchy. Then, she began replacing "Mr." with "Freddy." Thus, Freddy Fri was the name I decided to use. It was perfect! Now all I needed was a tagline. I thought about ways to incorporate hip-hop culture into the name. The result was: Freddy Fri, Your Pusha Man. The reference to "Your Pusha Man" is not about the drug game where it is normally heard. It reflects that I am pushing positivity and inspiration to help people become the best version of themselves.

After taking the necessary steps in getting started, Freddy Fri motivation was born. I began releasing videos every Wednesday and slowly started to rebrand myself. Playya 1000 was my hip hop persona and Freddy Fri Your Pusha Man stood for motivation and self-improvement. As my videos became more frequent and more popular, it felt like things just started to fall into place. At the time, I was following Eric Thomas religiously. When he announced that he was hosting a conference in Dallas, my wife and I decided to go. We got VIP passes and I had the opportunity to meet Eric Thomas himself and his right hand man, CJ. The most surreal part of the whole experience, however, was the fact that people knew me. Prior to the conference, I had become part of Eric Thomas's Breathe University. I would post videos in the Facebook group page. As a result, many people at the conference recognized me. They had seen my work, which resonated with them. It was an eye opening moment for me and it let me know that my videos were truly of value to others. I was totally amped!

I went back home from the conference knowing that I was on the right course. I was very humbled to know that people were enjoying my work. I kept working and refining my videos. Things went up a notch after Mr. Eric Thomas himself commented on one of my videos. He made the remark that he loved what I was doing and he encouraged me to keep moving forward. That blew me away! I was honored to receive that from him. Later, I received the opportunity to become part of the Game Changers Program. This was a program developed by Eric Thomas for aspiring motivational speakers. I was encouraged to attend the Game Changers conference in Atlanta and of course, my wife and I knew that we had to go. The entire event was amazing. There were tons of top-notch motivational speaking information, guest speakers and activities for the preparation needed to become a motivational speaker. The culmination of the event was Eric Thomas himself, the hip hop preacher addressing the crowd on the final day. Not only did he speak, but he also answered specific questions from the crowd. My wife and I were in the back row in a room filled with nearly three hundred people. Eric Thomas was speaking and everyone was tapped into his energy. You could literally hear a pin drop. At that moment, the craziest thing happened. Eric Thomas looked directly at me and quoted one of my lines: "You were born spectacular. It's in your DNA." If that wasn't enough to floor me, what he said next took the cake. He said, "Some of you speakers out there, I'm already feeling what you're doing." Then he looked directly at me and said, "Bro, I'm feeling your stuff." It was the most unreal moment. We couldn't believe it. My wife and I sat there with our jaws dropped wide open. I knew it had to be a sign.

After the speech, everyone was given the opportunity to sign up for the Game Changers program. The enrollment fee wasn't exactly cheap, which gave me pause. I kept thinking about performing as Playya 1000 and all the underground success we had achieved and yet still never became a household name. I had several opportunities back then to move to Los Angeles, New York or Atlanta for an opportunity to take my music to a higher level. However, I never left my hometown. I just wasn't ready. Now I felt that this was my opportunity to change that. After talking with my wife about it, she encouraged me move forward with my dreams. She told me that she believed in me and supported me. She also told me that I have a special gift that should be shared with the masses. That day, I became an official member of the Game Changers. I would eventually go on to become an Eric Thomas and Associates Certified Speaker. I learned how to secure gigs, how to produce a high-quality video and how to properly record and edit my video. I also learned about industry standard video recorders, quality microphones and how to present myself professionally. The Game Changers program also demonstrated how I can effectively promote my videos. I learned about what was required to become a superior professional speaker and about mastering the business side of motivational speaking. Soon after, I began receiving solicitations for paid speaking engagements.

I had been posting weekly videos for about a year when I noticed that several online motivational companies were posting voice-over videos, which were generating millions of views. The voice-over videos would feature a variety of speakers from Les Brown, Eric Thomas and Zig Ziglar to name a few. I thought to myself that I could do that kind of work. Immediately, I knew this was something to explore further. I reached out to my assistant, Desiree Brown and asked her to obtain information about becoming a featured voice over talent for some of the top companies. Desiree began sending my videos to various sites with large followings. For our first hit, we received an email back from a company called Fearless Motivation. They are one of the largest online motivational voiceover companies with well over two million subscribers on YouTube. In their email, they shared that my information had been reviewed and that they liked my work. They also included a link to a video and requested that I create something similar. The funny thing was, the link was a video of me! Clearly, my hip-hop style motivation was a unique twist that they enjoyed. I quickly began working with Fearless Motivation, which eventually led to me working with other companies such as Motiversity, Motivation 2 Study, and many others. So many doors opened for me simply because I had an idea and I followed through with it. I implore you to do the same. Do not wait, do not continue to think about it, just do it!

Now it is not uncommon to hear my voice featured in videos with the top motivational speakers in the world. I am included in the same voice-over videos with people such as Les Brown, Eric Thomas, Zig Ziglar and countless others. As of this writing, my voice is featured in well over three hundred million social media views and countless downloads and streams. However, the voice over video that I am most proud of is one where I am featured along with Denzel Washington, which is entitled "Say Thank You." This video itself has well over fifty million views on various social media platforms.

I am still friends with a number of guys from the original Game Changers class. We started a group called Lemon Squeeze. In this group, we bounce our motivational and business ideas off of one another and we challenge each other to enact the ideas that are feasible. Lemon Squeeze is the group that pushed me to start my next venture—the Student Athlete Success Series. At my basketball tournaments, I choose two teams and hold a talk about handling adversity in life and as a student athlete. Interestingly enough, this series has also served as a learning arena for me. Before starting, I would always use hip-hop as an icebreaker for my speeches to add shock value and get the audience excited. I would do a mini-performance at the beginning of an event rather than incorporating rap into the speeches themselves. However, it was through reaching out to one resistant player that I figured out an additional way of reaching and instilling positivity into the masses.

One young man's team had played a game in my tournament and they lost. It just so happened that the two teams that I chose for the Success Series that Saturday were this young man's team and their opponents. The last thing this kid wanted to do was come sit in a room with the opposing team and listen to me speak. I was just about to start our session when one his teammates told me that he was missing. Rather than joining the class with the rest of his team, he went and sat in the bleachers. He was mad at the world and insisted on not attending the Success Series. I went to talk to him. While sitting in the bleachers amongst the noise and crowd of people watching the current game, I told him that this was exactly why he needed to attend the session. I explained that he would learn how to deal with disappointment and adversity. When that didn't work, I recruited the other players from the classroom to the bleachers with me. There we all were, surrounding him with love in the stands. All of the players from his team and the opposing team encouraged him to come to the class. This young man eventually gave in and came to the classroom. I started my speech the usual way, with an attention grabbing, shock value rap. Everyone was engaged except for the angry young man. I asked the other student athletes if it would be okay to say another rap, especially for the mad young man. They all quickly screamed yes! Please do! This is the moment I figured out how to truly incorporate hip-hop into a motivational speech. All of my new raps were full of great teaching lyrics. When I started saying the rap dedicated to the troubled athlete, I would stop at every teachable point in the verse. I would explain its value in real-world terms. Then I'd say another few rhymes and repeat the process. Everyone loved it! By the end of my teaching session, the troubled kid was all smiles. I gave him a Make Every Day a Wins Day t-shirt and took pictures of him wearing the shirt. He became a stronger young man that day and in the process, I became a better speaker.

It was an entirely new approach to my motivational teaching process. I knew from then on, that I wanted to do things this way. I realized that I could take a sixteen bar rap and turn it into a thirty-minute presentation. I had finally figured out a way to fully incorporate my hip-hop into motivational speeches. This was a game changer for me! I kept posting videos on Facebook, Instagram, Twitter, and YouTube and suddenly people were messaging me, asking me to help them. I was changing people's lives and it felt amazing. After my videos gained traction, I started the WINSday Family Facebook group, where people from all over the world share their personal stories and tips to motivate and support one another. The goal is for us all to overcome obstacles and enjoy the life that has been given to us through living a positive existence.

Once you start doing things out of love and start pouring into the world unselfishly, the world will eventually start pouring back into you. As long as you figure out how to add value first, people will have no other option than to add value back into you. I tell my story to show others that they too can overcome just as I did. No matter what adversities are faced in life, you can come back and win in your game of life. This is what drives and motives me to continue creating empowering programs and videos, to be a personal/group life transformational consultant and coach. I am blessed to be one of very few speakers who has the ability to use the power of hip-hop to reach, teach, motivate, and inspire people of all ages, races, and ethnicities.

In essence, I'm teaching people to climb the hump of life's adversities and make every day a WINSday. I want everyone who reads this book to know that if I can overcome the hardships of my life, then so can you. Sometimes adjustments have to be made and that's okay. As long as you're still breathing, you still have an opportunity to be achieving. You can conquer any setback or failure no matter the circumstance. I am living proof that every life matters. Develop your personal game plan for success and begin taking the necessary steps to becoming the very best version of yourself. And soon you will find yourself on the other side of that hump making every day of your life a WINSday!

CHAPTER

(The W.I.N.S.D.A.Y Formula)

Now that you know my story, through all of its ups, downs, highs and lows, this book would not be complete without providing practical information, tools, tips and tricks to help you live a happy, fruitful life. By now, you know that my mission is to elicit a positive transformation within you. I developed the W.I.N.S.D.A.Y formula as a guide to help you overcome any adversity or turbulence in your life. Whenever you are facing a problem or dilemma, refer to this formula for resolution and resurgence. The W.I.N.S.D.A.Y formula is designed to ensure that you are winning every moment of every day, even if you feel like that particular day was a loss. Within each letter of the W.I.N.S.D.A.Y acronym, I share useful strategies in leading a victorious life. Your time is not next year or the next decade. Your time is now! Right now is the best time to make the necessary adjustments in your life to ensure a path of winning and success. Remember, we never lose; we learn. If a winning mindset is developed, victory can be achieved even in the toughest of times. Follow my formula for success:

- o **W** – Willingness to Work
- o **I** – Integrity Is Important
- o **N** – Never Negative
- o **S** – See Success
- o **D** – Daily Determination
- o **A** – Appetite for Ascension
- o **Y** - Yes You Can

WILLINGNESS TO WORK

To succeed in life, you must have an internal drive and a willingness to work. Others can plant the seed in you, but it is you who must water it! Watering that seed regularly results in growth. Without a willingness to work, no goal can be achieved and no plan can be executed. Thus, be sure to water your seeds on a daily basis! This can be done by putting in the work, consistently. Doing the small, seemingly insignificant things will open the doors of opportunity every time you knock!

The Parable of Two Basketball Players

There were two basketball players who began playing on one of my teams about the same time. Both of the players were in the seventh grade and possessed an equal level of experience. To improve their game, I constructed the same plan of action for them both. In addition to regular team practice, they were also required to refine their fundamental skills outside of the gym. This extra training was done at home, three days a week for an hour each time. Player one was totally committed. She gave 100% effort, attended all practices and diligently completed the extra home training each week. Player two displayed a lackluster effort level. She gave a mere 50% of her capabilities. To make matters worse, she frequently missed team practices and sporadically worked on her fundamental skills.

Both players started on the development team when they entered my basketball program. Within a year's time, player one had ascended to my elite team while player two remained on the development team. Player two never acquired the skills needed to play division one college basketball. Player one went on to realize her dream of playing division one college basketball.

It's very true that you get out of life what you put into it! You must make a commitment to your dreams and do the work to reach them, no matter how difficult. Eliminate the deterrents of your life like laziness, self-doubt and excuses. Put in the sweat equity and create an atmosphere of winning for your life! Success doesn't come easy. It requires a high degree of effort and unwavering commitment. If you are not achieving success at the level you desire, it's time for you to give more!

List 3 things that demonstrate your willingness to work in elevating your life:

1. _____

_____

_____

2. _____

_____

_____

3. _____

_____

_____

INTEGRITY IS IMPORTANT

Integrity is important because it is the building block of trust. Your integrity will create trust amongst others. Without integrity, trust will be virtually non-existent and others will always question your motives and behavior. On the other hand, being trustworthy brings about good deeds from others, respect and long-lasting, supportive relationships. Most of all, the universe will supernaturally yield a winning lifestyle upon you.

The BB Gun and Me

When I was twelve years old, my daddy surprised me with a brand new BB gun. I couldn't wait to show it off to one of my friends. He came to my house so we could play with the BB gun. We took turns shooting the gun at a tin can on the tree stump in my front yard. We made a $5 dollar bet to see who could shoot the can off the tree stump and make it flip the most times. It was my turn and I was intently locked in on the target. Then, I slowly pulled the trigger. What I heard next was not the sweet sound of "ping," that I expected, but instead it was a horrific sound of "crash."

That was the sound of my daddy's front window shattering to his brand new, hot rod car. Instantly, I went into panic mode. I couldn't tell my dad that I broke one of the windows on his precious, new car. To conceal my wrongdoing, I came up with the "unbrilliant idea" of pretending like I knew nothing about it. I made my friend swear to secrecy about it. When my daddy came home, he inspected the window and asked if I knew what happened. I stuck to my lack of integrity and uttered a convincing "no." He also asked my friend, who loyally followed my lead and denied having any knowledge about the broken window.

It was a few days later and I thought I had gotten away with my lack of integrity. Turns out that Ms. Pearl, an elderly woman who lived next door saw the entire incident. She snitched me out to my stepmom who, in turn, questioned me about it. I was caught red-handed and had no choice, but to tell my dad the truth. With reservations, I finally admitted to my dad that I was at fault for breaking his car window. Needless to say, he was furious! He sent me to my room and came inside shortly thereafter. Problem was, he wasn't alone. He had a friend with him: A thick, leather belt! I don't know if it was the sound of the car window breaking or the sound of the belt hitting my behind, but that story always comes to mind when I think of integrity! I will never forget what my dad said "if I had just told him the truth in the beginning, my punishment would have been less severe."

Are you lacking integrity? Do others find you trustworthy? Do you have morals and principles? Or, are you wielding a BB gun so to speak, with no real direction? I need you to put the BB gun down for good, as I did. Then I need you to create a culture of integrity in your life. I will give you the first step: Start by instilling good character within yourself.

What are some steps you can take in building and maintaining integrity?

1. _____

_____

_____

2. _____

_____

_____

3. _____

_____

_____

NEVER NEGATIVE

In the words of Henry Ford, "If you think you can or if you think you can't, you're probably right." So, please eliminate self-doubt and don't speak negativity into existence. Negativity breeds lack, failure and despondency. Alternatively, positivity results in optimism and encouragement. Developing a culture of winning is not possible when your life is bound by negativity. Let go of hopelessness and be proactive in attaining the awesome plans of your life. Surround yourself with positive people who support you in your dreams and goals.

Negative Nellies and Doubting Thomases

As a basketball coach, I have encountered all types of players who doubt themselves. These players suffer from a severe case of "stinking thinking" as the late, great Zig Ziglar calls it. Once, I coached a player who was consumed with poor self-confidence. I noticed that when she missed a shot during games, she would always say, "I suck, I'm horrible"! Of course, I didn't like her response. Your own words dictate who you are and she was clearly displaying destructive behavior. During a time out, I immediately engaged the player. I told her "You are a good basketball shooter and shooters believe in themselves"! At that time, we were losing the game by two points with only ten seconds left in the game. I purposely drew up a play up for her to shoot the last shot. I wanted to instill courage and signify that I believed in her.

Before the game went back into play, I said, "Listen, I need you to speak positive affirmations because on this team, we are never negative"! I also told her "I believe in you, your team believes in you and now I need you to believe in yourself"! The game resumed and emotions were running high. The player went to her correct position on the court and we executed the play perfectly. Unfortunately, she missed the shot. However, the basketball hit the front rim of the goal and bounced right back into her hands. There was only three seconds left in the game. She quickly shot the ball again and all I heard was swish! It was nothing but net!

Because she made the choice to release the negativity and believe in herself, she was given another opportunity to win.

Obviously, the crowd and our team went crazy! They mobbed her in all of their excitement. It was a teary-eyed moment. After that game, her self-confidence and self-esteem greatly improved. She learned a valuable lesson that will remain with her for the rest of her life. I hope her story compels you to eradicate negativity from your life and speak positivity into every aspect of your life. Believing in yourself will create the opportunity for you to hit the game winning shot of your life!

1. List at least 3 good qualities you possess?

_____

_____

_____

_____

_____

2. What are some things that make you happy?

_____

_____

_____

_____

_____

3. List 3 ways you can avoid negative thoughts and undisciplined behavior:

_____

_____

_____

_____

_____

SEE SUCCESS

To succeed, you must visualize yourself living an abundant life. Speak positive affirmations to yourself every day. Tell yourself that you can do this! Even if your plans are derailed, remain vigilant in seeking your goals and find a way to recapture the advantage in your game of life. Never give in to despair. Keep taking action to achieve your goals no matter how difficult the road may seem. There is always a silver lining in every rough patch.

Write the Ending First

Great movie producers are often asked the following question: What is the first thing you do when writing a movie script? Most of them answer by saying they always begin writing the script with the ending in mind. They visualize the ending of the movie first, then work backwards to input every detail leading up to the grand finale. That's exactly what you should do in your walk with life! In every aspect of your life, keep a mental picture of what success looks like. Thereafter, determine the steps that are needed to breathe life into that goal or dream. For example, a person who experiences a lay-off from their job must prepare to re-evaluate their employment options and livelihood. This is the perfect time for self-assessment and recognizing your passions in life. Next, the question that should be addressed is: What does career success look like for me? Whether you want to become a physician, attorney, business owner or learn a trade, it all begins with you seeing yourself as a success in that field.

1. What does success mean to you?

_____

_____

_____

_____

_____

2. List 3 steps that will help you in becoming more successful.

_____

_____

_____

_____

_____

3. List your top 3 goals in life and the needed steps to achieve them

_____

_____

_____

_____

_____

DAILY DETERMINATION

People always seem to find the energy to do the things that they like to do, even when they're dead tired. In contrast, people will often avoid taking the basic actions needed for success when met with difficulties or when extra effort is needed. Be mindful and diligent in everything you do! Daily determination will help you overcome a lack of energy. Refuse to lose and remain an unbreakable force!

What's Your "Why"?

Discovering your "why" gives you daily determination. Many people desire to be successful for personal gratification. However, always remember that your "why" will be much stronger if it goes beyond yourself. For instance, my "why" involves representing the legacy of my mama and providing for my family. Know the power of purpose! Learn to help others win as you are on your own journey of winning. When you do this, no obstacle is insurmountable and no dream or goal is out of your reach!

1. What is your passion?

_____

_____

_____

_____

_____

2. What is your purpose in life?

_____

_____

_____

_____

3. Write 3 "why's" that will inspire you to have daily determination.

_____

_____

_____

_____

_____

APPETITE FOR ASCENSION

You must be equipped with a burning desire to chase after your dreams and never let anyone stand in your way. There will be people in your life that will try to hold you down. Many times, those people are friends and family. Don't listen to the naysayers or self-doubt. Block out the noise of rejection and degradation. Maintain your objectives and refuse to lose! Use any negativity that comes your way as the fuel that drives your appetite for ascension.

Be Like Les Brown

A world renowned motivational speaker, the great Les Brown gives an impactful speech in which he talks about his aspirations of becoming a disc jockey. In efforts to achieve this ambition, he tells about applying for a job at his local radio station multiple times. He kept visiting the radio station until they finally hired him as an intern. He took full advantage of the opportunity and learned everything there was about being a disc jockey. Les got his big break when the "on air" disc jockey could not finish his show due to being inebriated. At the time, Les was the only other person at the station. In attempts to find a quick replacement, the owner of the station directed Les to make a few phone calls. Les did not become offended when the owner bypassed him as an option of managing the show. Instead, Les decided to demonstrate his specific talents and value. He knew it was his time to shine and there was absolutely no way he was calling on anyone else to run the show. Les convinced the owner to allow him to take over. The speech that Les gives in telling his story is nothing less than phenomenal. The passion in his voice is palpable. At the end of the speech, he enthusiastically proclaims, "I was hungry"! What is your appetite for ascension? I need you to be just like Les Brown and proclaim your hopes and dreams! For, you too can ascend to greatness!

1. What are your life goals and objectives?

_____

_____

_____

_____

_____

2. What are some ways that you can better prepare yourself to become what you want to be? Also, establish a timeline for your preparation:

_____

_____

_____

_____

_____

YES YOU CAN

You were born with success in your DNA. I'm not talking about Deoxyribonucleic acid. I am speaking of your "Dynamic Natural Ability," also known as your DNA. Your "Dynamic" is your "wow" factor. It is an inner glow; a positive energy that only you can release to the world. Your "Natural" is the thing that comes easy to you, but is difficult for most. Everyone has a "Natural" element that distinctly separates them from others. Finally, your "Ability" refers to your power or capacity to act physically and mentally. Basically, it is your "Ability" that allows you to take the action required to bring your dynamic and natural gifts to the world.

Know That You Are Worthy

Let me remind you that we are all human beings made of flesh and blood. The people achieving next level success are not robots or Martians. In fact, they are normal everyday people. My cousin Willie is a regular person with many talents. One of his obvious gifts is making people laugh. He's naturally funny. He doesn't have to work hard at it or try to convince others that he is funny. He just is! It's always a blast being around him because his mood is always light and full of laughter. For years, Darrell and I have been trying to get him to become a stand-up comedian. Even though he is uniquely talented, he had a fear of performing in front of an audience.

Using my personal talents to motivate him, I was unrelenting. I constantly told him how great he was, how he could use his talent to touch the lives of others and not to mention, how being a stand-up comedian could propel his livelihood. He finally accepted my encouragements and started taking classes for beginner comedians. After a few class sessions, he eventually performed in front of a live audience. I was there to provide support and cheer him on. The response from the crowd was overwhelmingly positive. He performed like a veteran comedian. In fact, many people were in awe that it was his very first performance.

Willie was met with a high level of success because he was operating in his natural gift. Sometimes, the world will see your "natural" before you do. When people say things like "Wow, you're smart! You're fast, you're charismatic, you're very well spoken," they are providing hints about your "Natural" gift. Please understand that a major key to overall happiness in life is figuring out what you're naturally good at and finding a way to make a living at it! Willie finally put forth his DNA and emerged triumphant. You too can achieve at a higher level, but you must believe!

In the space below, I want you to state your dreams. Next write, what you think is stopping you from achieving your dreams. Then, write what makes you uncomfortable in the pursuit of your dreams. Finally, write the changes that need to occur that will lead you to the doorsteps of your dreams.

1. What is your dream?

_____

_____

_____

_____

_____

_____

2. What do you think is stopping you from achieving your dream?

_____

_____

_____

_____

_____

_____

3. What about the pursuit of your dream makes you uncomfortable?

_____

_____

_____

_____

_____

_____

4. What do you need to change in your life to get closer to achieving your dream?

_____

_____

_____

_____

_____

_____

Life innately comes with its challenges and roadblocks. Those who look beyond the obstacles will smell the aroma of sweet victory in reaching their goals and dreams. Those who relent to the pressures of life may find themselves wallowing in mediocrity. Be deliberate in your actions in becoming the best version of yourself. Utilize the W.I.N.S.D.A.Y formula on a daily basis in every aspect of your life. Committing to the process will help open the doors of opportunity in your journey. Do not fret about the possibility of failure. Temporary setbacks are a necessity. Growth and maturity results from what many people define as a failure. Do not be misguided in this. Rather, use these moments as encouragement to keep moving forward.

From the W.I.N.S.D.A.Y formula, you have all of the tools needed to be great and elevate. Now is the time for you to take action to overcome your fears and doubts. Believe in yourself, discover your gift and your purpose and map out a course of action. Execute your established actions, fail, revise, execute, fail again, revise again and keep repeating. Failure is not failure in the sense of defeat. Failure is part of life's plan. It is the path to success. It's the preparation for the evolutionary ride of your life. Giving up is not an option. Remember that our internal GPS is set at the destination of next level. Stay the course, follow the formula and climb the hump of adversity to make every day of the rest of your life a WINSday!